Modern Critical Interpretations

William Faulkner's
The Sound and the Fury

Bloom's Modern Critical Interpretations

Adventures of
   Huckleberry Finn
All Quiet on the
   Western Front
Animal Farm
Beloved
Beowulf
Billy Budd, Benito
   Cereno, Bartleby
   the Scrivener, and
   Other Tales
The Bluest Eye
Brave New World
Cat on a Hot Tin Roof
The Catcher in the Rye
Catch-22
Cat's Cradle
The Color Purple
Crime and
   Punishment
The Crucible
Daisy Miller, The
   Turn of the Screw,
   and Other Tales
David Copperfield
Death of a Salesman
The Divine Comedy
Don Quixote
Dracula
Dubliners
Emma
Fahrenheit 451
A Farewell to Arms
Frankenstein
The General Prologue
   to the Canterbury
   Tales
The Glass Menagerie
The Grapes of Wrath
Great Expectations
The Great Gatsby
Gulliver's Travels

Hamlet
The Handmaid's Tale
Heart of Darkness
I Know Why the
   Caged Bird Sings
The Iliad
The Interpretation of
   Dreams
Invisible Man
Jane Eyre
The Joy Luck Club
Julius Caesar
The Jungle
King Lear
Long Day's Journey
   Into Night
Lord of the Flies
The Lord of the Rings
Macbeth
The Merchant of Venice
The Metamorphosis
A Midsummer Night's
   Dream
Moby-Dick
My Ántonia
Native Son
Night
1984
The Odyssey
Oedipus Rex
The Old Man and
   the Sea
One Flew Over the
   Cuckoo's Nest
One Hundred Years
   of Solitude
Othello
Paradise Lost
The Pardoner's Tale
A Portrait of the Artist
   as a Young Man
Pride and Prejudice

Ragtime
The Red Badge
   of Courage
The Rime of the
   Ancient Mariner
Romeo & Juliet
The Scarlet Letter
A Scholarly Look at
   The Diary of
   Anne Frank
A Separate Peace
Silas Marner
Slaughterhouse-Five
Song of Myself
Song of Solomon
The Sonnets of
   William Shakespeare
Sophie's Choice
The Sound and
   the Fury
The Stranger
A Streetcar Named
   Desire
Sula
The Sun Also Rises
A Tale of Two Cities
The Tales of Poe
The Tempest
Tess of the
   D'Urbervilles
Their Eyes Were
   Watching God
Things Fall Apart
To Kill a Mockingbird
Waiting for Godot
Walden
The Waste Land
White Noise
Wuthering Heights

Modern Critical Interpretations

William Faulkner's
The Sound and the Fury

Edited and with an introduction by

Harold Bloom
Sterling Professor of the Humanities
Yale University

Chelsea House Publishers
PHILADELPHIA

The Chelsea House World Wide Web address is
http: //www.chelseahouse.com

Printed and bound in the United States of America

10   9   8   7

∞ The paper used in this publication meets the minimum
requirements of the American National Standard for
Permanence of Paper for Printed Library Materials,
Z39.48-1984.

Library of Congress Cataloging-in-Publication Data
William Faulkner's The sound and the fury / edited
and with an introduction by Harold Bloom.
       p.   cm. — (Modern critical interpretations)
   Bibliography: p.
   Includes index.
   ISBN 1-55546-042-9 (alk. paper): $24.50
   1. Faulkner, William, 1897–1962. Sound and the
fury. I. Bloom, Harold. II. Series.
PS3511.A86S865   1988   87-18366
813'.52—dc19   CIP

Contents

Editor's Note

This book brings together a representative selection of the best critical interpretations of William Faulkner's novel *The Sound and the Fury*. The critical essays are reprinted in the chronological sequence of their original publication. I am grateful to James Swenson and Paul Barickman for their assistance in editing this volume.

My introduction meditates upon the relation of *The Sound and the Fury* to Faulkner's anxieties, both literary and psychosexual. John T. Irwin begins the chronological sequence of criticism with an analysis of the narcissistic doubling that occurs in the course of Quentin's last day of life.

In Donald M. Kartiganer's exegesis, there is an emphasis upon the fragments of voices and perspectives that the novel tests and finds wanting. Gary Lee Stonum centers upon Faulkner's discovery, in writing *The Sound and the Fury*, that he can construct a narrative out of concerns that normally engage the poetic rather than the novelistic sensibility.

The vexed question of Faulkner's tragic vision is summed up by Warwick Wadlington, who argues that the novel's catharsis is brought about through Dilsey and the Easter sermon, rather than by Quentin's suicide. Thadious M. Davis, rather problematically, finds in *The Sound and the Fury*'s fragmented monologues and characters an inevitable structural metaphor for life that endures the cultural stratifications of a Jim Crow regime.

A Derrida-inspired deconstruction by John T. Matthews attempts to determine how—in Benjy's and Quentin's narratives—it is Caddy's absence that generates language, a language that seeks to restitute for Caddy's lost presence. Gail L. Mortimer describes Quentin's narrative in the Bergsonian terms that influenced Faulkner's obsession with the transience of time.

This book culminates in Eric J. Sundquist's polemic against the argument, originated by Faulkner himself and developed by his critics, that valorizes *The Sound and the Fury*'s Oedipal obsessions over its cultural concerns. Instead, Sundquist regards the Oedipal as a mask for Faulkner's true subject, the South's doom, racial hatred and compulsive reactions to miscegenation.

Introduction

I

No critic need invent William Faulkner's obsessions with what Nietzsche might have called the genealogy of the imagination. Recent critics of Faulkner, including David Minter, John T. Irwin, David M. Wyatt and Richard H. King, have emphasized the novelist's profound need to believe himself to have been his own father, in order to escape not only the Freudian family romance and literary anxieties of influence, but also the cultural dilemmas of what King terms "the Southern family romance." From *The Sound and the Fury* through the debacle of *A Fable*, Faulkner centers upon the sorrows of fathers and sons, to the disadvantage of mothers and daughters. No feminist critic ever will be happy with Faulkner. His brooding conviction that female sexuality is closely allied with death seems essential to all of his strongest fictions. It may even be that Faulkner's rhetorical economy, his wounded need to get his cosmos into a single sentence, is related to his fear that origin and end might prove to be one. Nietzsche prophetically had warned that origin and end were separate entities, and for the sake of life had to be kept apart, but Faulkner (strangely like Freud) seems to have known that the only Western trope participating neither in origin nor end is the image of the father.

By universal consent of critics and common readers, Faulkner now is recognized as the strongest American novelist of this century, clearly surpassing Hemingway and Fitzgerald, and standing as an equal in the sequence that includes Hawthorne, Melville, Mark Twain and Henry James. Some critics might add Dreiser to this group; Faulkner himself curiously would have insisted upon Thomas Wolfe, a generous though dubious judgment. The American precursor for Faulkner was Sherwood Anderson, but perhaps only as an impetus; the true American forerunner is the poetry of T. S. Eliot, as Judith L. Sensibar demonstrates. But the truer precursor for Faulk-

1

ner's fiction is Conrad, inescapable for the American novelists of Faulkner's generation, including Hemingway and Fitzgerald. Comparison to Conrad is dangerous for any novelist, and clearly Faulkner did not achieve a *Nostromo*. But his work of the decade 1929–39 does include four permanent books: *The Sound and the Fury, As I Lay Dying, Light in August,* and *Absalom, Absalom!* If one adds *Sanctuary* and *The Wild Palms,* and *The Hamlet* and *Go Down, Moses* in the early forties, then the combined effect is extraordinary.

From Malcolm Cowley on, critics have explained this effect as the consequence of the force of mythmaking, at once personal and local. Cleanth Brooks, the rugged final champion of the New Criticism, essentially reads Faulkner as he does Eliot's *The Waste Land,* finding the hidden God of the normative Christian tradition to be the basis for Faulkner's attitude towards nature. Since Brooks calls Faulkner's stance Wordsworthian, and finds Wordsworthian nature a Christian vision also, the judgment involved necessarily has its problematical elements. Walter Pater, a critic in a very different tradition, portrayed a very different Wordsworth in terms that seem to me not inapplicable to Faulkner:

> Religious sentiment, consecrating the affections and natural regrets of the human heart, above all, that pitiful awe and care for the perishing human clay, of which relic-worship is but the corruption, has always had much to do with localities, with the thoughts which attach themselves to actual scenes and places. Now what is true of it everywhere, is truest of it in those secluded valleys where one generation after another maintains the same abiding place; and it was on this side, that Wordsworth apprehended religion most strongly. Consisting, as it did so much, in the recognition of local sanctities, in the habit of connecting the stones and trees of a particular spot of earth with the great events of life, till the low walls, the green mounds, the half-obliterated epitaphs seemed full of voices, and a sort of natural oracle, the very religion of those people of the dales, appeared but as another link between them and the earth, and was literally a religion of nature.

A kind of stoic natural religion pervades this description, something close to the implicit faith of old Isaac McCaslin in *Go Down, Moses.* It seems unhelpful to speak of "residual Christianity" in Faulkner, as Cleanth Brooks does. Hemingway and Fitzgerald, in their nostalgias, perhaps were closer to a Christian ethos than Faulkner was in his great phase. Against current critical judgment, I prefer *As I Lay Dying* and *Light in August* to *The Sound and the Fury* and *Absalom, Absalom!* partly because the first two are more primordial in their vision, closer to the stoic intensities of their author's kind of natural piety. There is an *otherness* in Lena Grove and the Bundrens that would have moved Wordsworth, that is, the Wordsworth of *The Tale of Margaret, Michael,* and *The Old Cumberland Beggar.* A curious movement that is also a stasis becomes Faulkner's pervasive trope for Lena. Though he invokes the imagery of Keats's urn, Faulkner seems to have had the harvest-girl of Keats's *To Autumn* more in mind, or even the stately figures of the *Ode to Indolence.* We remember Lena Grove as stately, calm, a person yet a process, a serene and patient consciousness, full of wonder, too much a unitary being to need even her author's variety of stoic courage.

The uncanniness of this representation is exceeded by the Bundrens, whose plangency testifies to Faulkner's finest rhetorical achievement. *As I Lay Dying* may be the most original novel ever written by an American. Obviously it is not free of the deepest influence Faulkner knew as a novelist. The language is never Conradian, and yet the sense of the reality principle is. But there is nothing in Conrad like Darl Bundren, not even in *The Secret Agent. As I Lay Dying* is Faulkner's strongest protest against the facticity of literary convention, against the force of the familial past, which tropes itself in fiction as the repetitive form of narrative imitating prior narrative. The book is a sustained nightmare, insofar as it is Darl's book, which is to say, Faulkner's book, or the book of his daemon.

II

Canonization is a process of enshrining creative misinterpretations, and no one need lament this. Still, one element that ensues from this process all too frequently is the not very creative misinterpretation in which the idiosyncratic is distorted into the normative. Churchwardenly critics who assimilate the Faulkner of the Thirties to spiritual, social, and moral orthodoxy can and do assert Faulkner himself as their preceptor. But this is the Faulkner of the Fifties, Nobel laureate, State Department envoy and author of *A Fable*, a book of badness simply astonishing for Faulkner. The best of the normative critics, Cleanth Brooks, reads even *As I Lay Dying* as a quest for community, an exaltation of the family, an affirmation of Christian values. The Bundrens manifestly constitute one of the most terrifying visions of the family romance in the history of literature. But their extremism is not eccentric in the 1929–39 world of Faulkner's fiction. That world is founded upon a horror of families, a limbo of outcasts, an evasion of all values other than stoic endurance. It is a world in which what is silent in the other Bundrens speaks in Darl, what is veiled in the Compsons is uncovered in Quentin. So tangled are these returns of the repressed with what continues to be estranged that phrases like "the violation of the natural" and "the denial of the human" become quite meaningless when applied to Faulkner's greater fictions. In that world, the natural is itself a violation and the human already a denial. Is the weird quest of the Bundrens a violation of the natural, or is it what Blake would have called a terrible triumph for the selfish virtues of the natural heart? Darl judges it to be the latter, but Darl luminously denies the sufficiency of the human, at the cost of what seems schizophrenia.

Marxist criticism of imaginative literature, if it had not regressed abominably in our country, so that now it is a travesty of the dialectical suppleness of Adorno and Benjamin, would find a proper subject in the difficult relationship between the 1929 business panic and *As I Lay Dying*. Perhaps the self-destruction of our delusive political economy helped free Faulkner from whatever inhibitions, communal and personal, had kept him earlier from a saga like that of the Bundrens. Only an authentic seer can give permanent form to a prophecy like *As I Lay Dying*, which puts severely into question every received notion we have of the natural and the human. Darl asserts he has no mother, while taunting his enemy brother, Jewel, with the insistence that Jewel's mother was a horse. Their little brother, Vardaman, says: "My mother is a fish." The mother, dead and undead, is uncannier even than these children, when she confesses the truth of her existence, her rejecting vision of her children:

> I could just remember how my father used to say that the reason
> for living was to get ready to stay dead a long time. And when
> I would have to look at them day after day, each with his and
> her single and selfish thought, and blood strange to each other
> blood and strange to mine, and think that this seemed to be the
> only way I could get ready to stay dead, I would hate my father
> for having ever planted me. I would look forward to the times
> when they faulted, so I could whip them. When the switch fell
> I could feel it upon my flesh; when it welted and ridged it was
> my blood that ran, and I would think with each blow of the
> switch: Now you are aware of me! Now I am something in
> your secret and selfish life, who have marked your blood with
> my own for ever and ever.

This veritable apocalypse of any sense of otherness is no mere "denial of community." Nor are the Bundrens any "mimesis of essential nature."

They are a super-mimesis, an over-representation mocking nature while shadowing it. What matters in major Faulkner is that the people have gone back, not to nature but to some abyss before the Creation-Fall. Eliot insisted that Joyce's imagination was eminently orthodox. This can be doubted, but in Faulkner's case there is little sense in baptizing his imagination. One sees why he preferred reading the Old Testament to the New, remarking that the former was stories and the latter, ideas. The remark is inadequate except insofar as it opposes Hebraic to Hellenistic representation of character. There is little that is Homeric about the Bundrens, or Sophoclean about the Compsons. Faulkner's irony is neither classical nor romantic, neither Greek nor German. It does not say one thing while meaning another, nor trade in contrasts between expectation and fulfillment. Instead, it juxtaposes incommensurable realities: of self and other, of parent and child, of past and future. When Gide maintained that Faulkner's people lacked souls, he simply failed to observe that Faulkner's ironies were Biblical. To which an amendment must be added. In Faulkner, only the ironies are Biblical. What Faulkner's people lack is the blessing; they cannot contend for a time without boundaries. Yahweh will make no covenant with them. Their agon therefore is neither the Greek one for the foremost place nor the Hebrew one for the blessing, which honors the father and the mother. Their agon is the hopeless one of waiting for their doom to lift.

III

The Sound and the Fury always moved Faulkner to tenderness, far more than his other novels. It was for him a kind of Keatsian artifact, vase or urn invested with a permanent aesthetic dignity. His judgment has prevailed with his critics, though some doubts and reservations have been voiced. Like *Absalom, Absalom!*, *The Sound and the Fury* seems to me a lesser work than *Light in August,* or than *As I Lay Dying,* which is Faulkner's masterwork. The mark of Joyce's *Ulysses* is a little too immediate on *The Sound and the Fury,* which does not always sustain its intense rhetoricity, its anguished word-consciousness. There is something repressed almost throughout *The Sound and the Fury,* some autobiographical link between Quentin's passion for his sister Caddy and a nameless passion of Faulkner's, perhaps (as David Minter surmises) for the sister he never had, perhaps his desire for Estelle Oldham, later to be his wife, but only after being married to another. Jealousy, intimately allied to the fear of mortality, is a central element in *The Sound and the Fury.*

Hugh Kenner, comparing Faulkner's novel to its precursors by Conrad and Joyce, dismisses the Compson family saga as excessively arty. The judgment is cruel, yet cogent if Joyce and Conrad are brought too close, and Faulkner does not distance himself enough from them. This makes for an unhappy paradox; *The Sound and the Fury* is a little too elaborately wrought to sustain its rather homely substance, its plot of family disasters. But that substance, those familial disorders, are entirely too available to Freudian and allied reductions; such repetitions and doublings are prevalent patterns, vicissitudes of drives too dismally universal truly to serve novelistic ends. Only Jason, of all the Compsons, is individual enough to abide as an image in the reader's memory. His Dickensian nastiness makes Jason an admirable caricature, while Quentin, Caddy, and Benjy blend into the continuum, figures of thought for whom Faulkner has failed to find the inevitable figures of speech.

Faulkner's Appendix for *The Sound and the Fury*, written for Malcolm Cowley's *The Portable Faulkner*, not only has become part of the novel, but famously constitutes the definitive interpretation of the novel, or Faulkner's will-to-power over his own text. The Appendix is very much Faulkner the yarn-spinner of 1946, soon to write such feebler works as *Intruder in the Dust, Knight's Gambit,* and *Requiem for a Nun,* before collapsing into the disaster of *A Fable.* It is not the Faulkner of 1928, commencing his major phase, and yet the Appendix does have a curious rhetorical authority, culminating in Faulkner's tribute to the blacks (after simply listing Dilsey's name, since she is beyond praise): "They endured." Sadly, this is an authority mostly lacking in the actual text of *The Sound and the Fury.* Quentin's voice makes me start when it is too clearly the voice of Stephen Daedalus, and Joyce's medley of narrative voices fades in and out of Faulkner's story with no clear relation to Faulkner's purposes. Only Poldy, fortunately, is kept away, for his sublime presence would be sublimely irrelevant and so would sink the book.

I emphasize the limitations of *The Sound and the Fury* only because we are in danger of overlooking them, now that Faulkner has become, rightly, our canonical novelist in this century, clearly our strongest author of prose fiction since the death of Henry James. *As I Lay Dying* was a radical experiment that worked magnificently; its forms and voices are apposite metaphors for the fierce and terrifying individualities of the Bundrens. *The Sound and the Fury* was also a remarkable experiment, but too derivative from Joyce's *Ulysses,* and perhaps too dark for Faulkner's own comfort.

What saves the Compson saga is that it is a saga; and finds a redeeming context in the reader's sense of larger significances that always seem to pervade Faulkner's major writings. We read *The Sound and the Fury* and we hear a tale signifying a great deal, because Faulkner constitutes for us a

literary cosmos of continual reverberations. Like Dilsey, we too are per-
suaded that we have seen the first and the last, the beginning and the ending
of a story that transcends the four Compson children, and the squalors of
their family romance.

Doubling and Incest / Repetition and Revenge

John T. Irwin

The narcissistic origin of doubling and the scenario of madness leading to the suicidal murder of the double help to illuminate the internal narrative of Quentin Compson's last day given in *The Sound and the Fury* and in turn to illuminate the story he tells in *Absalom, Absalom!* In the fictive time of the novels, Quentin and Shreve's joint narration, which occupies the last half of *Absalom*, takes place in January 1910, and Quentin's suicide occurs six months later on June 2, 1910, but the account of that suicide is given in a novel that appeared seven years before *Absalom*. Since we already know Quentin's end when we observe his attempt in *Absalom* to explain the reason for Bon's murder, we not only participate in that effort, but also engage at the same time in an analogous effort of our own to explain Quentin's murder of himself. And it is only when we see in the murder of Bon by Henry what Quentin saw in it—that Quentin's own situation appears to be a repetition of the earlier story—that we begin to understand the reason for Quentin's suicide. And this whole repetitive structure is made even more problematic by the fact that the explanation which Quentin gives for Bon's murder (that Bon is black, i.e., the shadow self) may well be simply the return of the repressed—simply an unconscious projection of Quentin's own psychic history. Quentin's situation becomes endlessly repetitive insofar as he constantly creates the predecessors of that situation in his narration of past events. And to escape from that kind of repetition, one must escape from the self.

Like Narcissus, Quentin drowns himself, and the internal narrative of his last day, clearly the narrative of someone who has gone insane, is dominated by Quentin's obsessive attempts to escape from his shadow, to "trick his shadow," as he says. When Quentin leaves his dormitory on the morning of his death, the pursuit begins: "The shadow hadn't quite cleared the stoop. I stopped inside the door, watching the shadow move. It moved almost perceptibly, creeping back inside the door, driving the shadow back into the door. . . . The shadow on the stoop was gone. I stepped into the sunlight, finding my shadow again. I walked down the steps just ahead of it." Later, standing by the river, he looks down: "The shadow of the bridge, the tiers of railing, my shadow leaning flat upon the water, so easily had I tricked it that it would not quit me. At least fifty feet it was, and if I only had something to blot it into the water, holding it until it was drowned, the shadow of the package like two shoes wrapped up lying on the water. Niggers say a drowned man's shadow was watching him in the water all the time." Like Narcissus staring at his image in the pool, Quentin stares at his shadow in the river and significantly, makes a reference to Negroes in relation to that shadow. I say "significantly" because at crucial points during Quentin's last day this connection between the shadow and the Negro recurs, most notably on the train ride down to the river when Quentin sits next to a black man: "I used to think that a Southerner had to be always conscious of niggers. I thought that Northerners would expect him to. When I first came East I kept thinking You've got to remember to think of them as coloured people not niggers, and if it hadn't happened that I wasn't thrown with many of them, I'd have wasted a lot of time and trouble before I learned that the best way to take all people, black or white, is to take them for what they think they are, then leave them alone. That was when I realised that a nigger is not a person so much as a form of behaviour; a sort of obverse reflection of the white people he lives among." If, in Quentin's mind, blacks are the "obverse reflection" of whites, if they are like shadows, then in Quentin's narrative projection of his own psychodrama in *Absalom*, Charles Bon's role as the dark seducer, as the shadow self, is inevitably linked with Bon's Negro blood. Further, since Quentin's own shadow has Negro resonances in his mind, it is not surprising that on the day of his suicide Quentin, who is being pursued by his shadow, is told by one of the three boys that he meets walking in the country that he (Quentin) talks like a colored man, nor is it surprising that another of the boys immediately asks the first one if he isn't afraid that Quentin will hit him.

If Quentin's determination to drown his shadow represents the substitutive punishment, upon his own person, of the brother seducer (the dark self, the ego shadowed by the unconscious) by the brother avenger (the bright self, the ego controlled by the superego), then it is only appropriate that the events from Quentin's past that obsessively recur during the internal narrative leading up to his drowning are events that emphasize Quentin's failure as both brother avenger and brother seducer in relation to his sister Candace—failures which his drowning of himself is meant to redeem. On the one hand, Quentin is haunted by his inability to kill Candace's lover Dalton Ames and by his further inability to prevent Candace from marrying Herbert Head, whom he knows to be a cheat. But on the other hand, he is equally tormented by his own failure to commit incest with his sister. In this connection it is significant that one of the obsessive motifs in the narrative of Quentin's last day is the continual juxtaposition of Quentin's own virginity to his sister's loss of virginity: "In the South you are ashamed of being a virgin. Boys. Men. They lie about it. Because it means less to women, Father said. He said it was men invented virginity not women. Father said it's like death: only a state in which the others are left and I said, But to believe it doesn't matter and he said, That's what's so sad about anything: not only virginity, and I said, Why couldn't it have been me and not her who is unvirgin and he said, That's why that's sad too; nothing is even worth the changing of it."

In Quentin's world young men lose their virginity as soon as possible, but their sisters keep their virginity until they are married. The reversal of this situation in the case of Quentin and Candace makes Quentin feel that his sister has assumed the masculine role and that he has assumed the feminine role. Quentin's obsessive concern with Candace's loss of virginity is a displaced concern with his own inability to lose his virginity, for, as both novels clearly imply, Quentin's virginity is psychological impotence. Approaching manhood, Quentin finds himself unable to assume the role of a man. Consider his failure as the avenging brother when he encounters Dalton Ames on the bridge—Ames whom Quentin has earlier associated with the figure of the shadow. He tells Ames to leave town by sundown or he will kill him. Ames replies by drawing a pistol and demonstrating his marksmanship. He then offers the pistol to Quentin:

> youll need it from what you said Im giving you this one
> because youve seen what itll do
> to hell with your gun
> I hit him I was still trying to hit him long after he was holding
> my wrists but I still tried then it was like I was looking at him

through a piece of coloured glass I could hear my blood and
then I could see the sky again and branches against it and the
sun slanting through them and he holding me on my feet
  did you hit me
  I couldnt hear
  what
  yes how do you feel
  all right let go
  he let me go I leaned against the rail

Later, sick and ashamed, Quentin thinks, "I knew he hadnt hit me that he
had lied about that for her sake too and that I had just passed out like a
girl." Quentin, by rejecting the use of the pistol with its phallic significance
and thus avoiding the necessity of risking his life to back up his words,
relinquishes the masculine role of avenging brother and finds suddenly that
in relation to the seducer he has shifted to a feminine role. Struggling in
Ames's grasp, Quentin faints "like a girl," and Ames, because he sees the
sister in the brother, refuses to hurt Quentin and even lies to keep from
humiliating him.

    Quentin's failure of potency in the role of avenging brother is a repe-
tition of an earlier failure in the role of brother seducer. On that occasion,
Quentin had gone looking for Candace, suspecting that she had slipped
away to meet Dalton Ames, and he found her lying on her back in the
stream: "I ran down the hill in that vacuum of crickets like a breath travelling
across a mirror she was lying on her back in the water her head on the sand
spit the water flowing about her skirt half saturated flopped along her flanks
to the water motion in heavy ripples going nowhere." Forcing Candace to
get out of the water, Quentin begins to question her about Ames, only to
find that the questioning suddenly turns to the subject of his own virginity:

  Caddy you hate him dont you
  she moved my hand up against her throat her heart was hammering there . . .
  Yes I hate him I would die for him I've already died for him
I die for him over and over again everytime this goes . . .
  poor Quentin
  she leaned back on her arms her hands locked about her knees
  youve never done that have you
  what done what
  that what I have what I did
  yes yes lots of times with lots of girls

then I was crying her hand touched me again and I was crying
against her damp blouse then she lying on her back looking past
my head into the sky I could see a rim of white under her irises
I opened my knife

do you remember the day damuddy died when you sat down
in the water in your drawers

yes

I held the point of the knife at her throat

it wont take but a second just a second then I can do mine I
can do mine then

all right can you do yours by yourself

yes the blades long enough Benjys in bed by now

yes

it wont take but a second Ill try not to hurt

all right

will you close your eyes

no like this youll have to push it harder

touch your hand to it

but she didnt move her eyes were wide open looking past my
head at the sky

Caddy do you remember how Dilsey fussed at you because
your drawers were muddy

dont cry

Im not crying Caddy

push it are you going to

do you want me to

yes push it

touch your hand to it

dont cry poor Quentin . . .

what is it what are you doing

her muscles gathered I sat up

its my knife I dropped it

she sat up

what time is it

I dont know

she rose to her feet I fumbled along the ground

Im going let it go

I could feel her standing there I could smell her damp clothes
feeling her there

its right here somewhere

> let it go you can find it tomorrow come on
> wait a minute I'll find it
> are you afraid to
> here it is it was right here all the time
> was it come on . . .
>   its funny how you can sit down and drop something and have
> to hunt all around for it

Candace says that she has died for her lover many times, but for the narcissistic Quentin the mention of sexual death evokes the threat of real death, the feared dissolution of the ego through sexual union with another, the swallowing up of the ego in the instinctual ocean of the unconscious. And Quentin, tormented by his virginity, by his impotence ("poor Quentin youve never done that have you"), can only reply to Candace's sexual death by offering a real *liebestod*. He puts his knife to his sister's throat and proposes that they be joined forever in a murder/suicide—a double killing that represents the equivalent, on the level of brother/sister incest, of the suicidal murder of the brother seducer by the brother avenger. For if the brother-seducer/brother-avenger relationship represents doubling and the brother/sister relationship incest, then the brother/brother relationship is also a kind of incest and the brother/sister relationship a kind of doubling. In at least one version of the Narcissus myth (Pausanias), Narcissus is rendered inconsolable by the death of his identical twin sister, and when he sees himself reflected in the water he transfers to his own image the love that he felt for his dead twin. In this light, consider once again the image that begins the scene: Quentin says, "I ran down the hill in that vacuum of crickets like a breath travelling across a mirror she was lying on her back in the water" The narcissistic implication is that his sister lying on her back in the stream is like a mirror image of himself, and indeed, one of the recurring motifs in Quentin's internal narrative is the image of his sister in her wedding dress running toward him out of a mirror. Further, Quentin says that Ames was always "looking at me through her like through a piece of coloured glass."

It would appear that for Quentin the double as a male figure is associated with the shadow and the double as a female figure is associated with the mirror image. If so, then his suicide represents the attempt to merge those two images. During his walk in the country on the afternoon of his death, Quentin senses the nearness of a river and suddenly the smell of water evokes a memory of his desire for his sister and his desire for death:

> The draft in the door smelled of water, a damp steady breath.
> Sometimes I could put myself to sleep saying that over and over

until after the honeysuckle got all mixed up in it the whole thing came to symbolise night and unrest I seemed to be lying neither asleep nor awake looking down a long corridor of grey halflight where all stable things had become shadowy paradoxical all I had done shadows all I had felt suffered taking visible form antic and perverse mocking without relevance inherent themselves with the denial of the significance they should have affirmed thinking I was I was not who was not was not who.

I could smell the curves of the river beyond the dusk and I saw the last light supine and tranquil upon tideflats like pieces of broken mirror. . . . Benjamin the child of. How he used to sit before that mirror. Refuge unfailing in which conflict tempered silenced reconciled.

The image of Benjamin, Quentin's idiot younger brother, staring at himself in a mirror, locked forever in mental childhood, is a forceful evocation of the infantile, regressive character of narcissism, and it is in light of that infantile, regressive character that we can understand Quentin's drowning of himself in the river as an attempt to merge the shadow and the mirror image. Quentin's narcissism is, in Freudian terms, a fixation in secondary narcissism, a repetition during a later period in life (usually adolescence) of that primary narcissism that occurs between the sixth and the eighteenth months, wherein the child first learns to identify with its image and thus begins the work that will lead to the constitution of the ego as the image of the self and the object of love. The fixation in secondary narcissism in which the ego at a later period is recathected as the *sole* object of love condemns the individual to an endless repetition of an infantile state. This attempt to make the subject the sole object of its own love, to merge the subject and the object in an internal love union, reveals the ultimate goal of all infantile, regressive tendencies, narcissism included: it is the attempt to return to a state in which subject and object did not yet exist, to a time before that division occurred out of which the ego sprang—in short, to return to the womb, to reenter the waters of birth. But the desire to return to the womb is the desire for incest. Thus, Quentin's narcissism is necessarily linked with his incestuous desire for his sister, for as Otto Rank points out, brother-sister incest is a substitute for child-parent incest—what the brother seeks in his sister is his mother. And we see that the triangle of sister/brother-avenger/brother-seducer is a substitute for the Oedipal triangle of mother/father/son. Quentin's drowning of his shadow, then, is not only the punishment, upon his own person, of the brother seducer by the brother avenger, it is as well the union of the brother seducer with the sister, the union of Quentin's shadow with his mirror image in the water, the mirror image of himself that evokes his sister lying on her back in the stream. The punishment of the brother seducer by the brother avenger is death, but the union of the brother seducer and the sister is also death, for the attempt to merge the shadow and the mirror image results in the total immersion of both in the water on which they are reflected, the immersion of the masculine ego consciousness in the waters of its birth, in the womb of the feminine unconscious from which it was originally differentiated. By drowning his shadow, Quentin is able simultaneously to satisfy his incestuous desire and to punish it, and as we noted earlier it is precisely this simultaneous satisfaction and punishment of a repressed desire that is at the core of doubling. For Quentin, the incestuous union and the punishment of that union upon his own person can be accomplished by a single act because both the union and its punishment are a *liebestod*, a dying of the ego into the other.

In the confrontation between Quentin and Candace at the stream, this linking of sexual desire and death centers for Quentin around the image of Candace's muddy drawers and the death of their grandmother, "Damuddy." The image recalls an incident in their childhood when, during their grandmother's funeral, they had been sent away from the house to play. Candace goes wading in the stream, and when Quentin and Versh tell her that she'll get a whipping for getting her dress wet, she says that she'll take it off to let it dry, and she asks the black boy Versh to unbutton the back:

> "Don't you do it, Versh." Quentin said.
> "Taint none of my dress." Versh said.
> "You unbutton it, Versh." Caddy said, "Or I'll tell Dilsey what you did yesterday." So Versh unbuttoned it.
> "You just take your dress off." Quentin said. Caddy took her dress off and threw it on the bank. Then she didn't have on anything but her bodice and drawers, and Quentin slapped her and she slipped and fell down in the water.

Candace splashes water on Quentin, an act that in retrospect is sexually symbolic, and Quentin's fear that now they will both get a whipping destroys his attempt to play the role of the protective brother. Shifting from an active to a passive role, Quentin sees Caddy take charge and lead the children back to the house while he lags behind, taunted by Caddy. When they reach the house, Caddy climbs the tree outside the parlor window to see the funeral, and at that point the image of her muddy drawers seen by the children below is fused with the image of Damuddy's death. It is significant that Quentin's obsessive linking of these two images (his sexual desire for his sister and death) involves the repetition, in each case, of the same word—the word "muddy" in Candace's "muddy drawers" and "Damuddy's" funeral, for the threat that sexual union poses to the bright, narcissistic ego is, in Quentin's mind, associated with the image of mud—soft, dark, corrupt, enveloping—the image of being swallowed up by the earth. In the scene where Candace interrupts an abortive sexual encounter in the barn between Quentin and a girl named Natalie ("a dirty girl like Natalie," as Candace says), Quentin retaliates by jumping into the hog wallow and then smearing his sister with mud:

> *She had her back turned I went around in front of her. You know what I was doing? She turned her back I went around in front of her the rain creeping into the mud flatting her bodice through her dress it smelled horrible. I was hugging her that's what I was doing. . . .*
>
> *I dont give a damn what you were doing*
>
> *You dont you dont I'll make you I'll make you give a damn. She hit my hands away I smeared mud on her with the other hand I couldn't feel the wet smacking of her hand I wiped mud from my legs smeared it on her wet hard turning body hearing her fingers going into my face but I couldn't feel it even when the rain began to taste sweet on my lips . . .*
>
> *We lay in the wet grass panting the rain like cold shot on my back. Do you care now do you do you*
>
> *My Lord we sure are in a mess get up. Where the rain touched my forehead it began to smart my hand came red away streaking off pink in the rain. Does it hurt*
>
> *Of course it does what do you reckon*
>
> *I tried to scratch your eyes out my Lord we sure do stink we better try to wash it off in the branch.*

Later, when Quentin identifies with his sister's lover Dalton Ames and imagines Ames and Candace making "the beast with two backs," the image of Quentin and Candace smeared with mud from the hog wallow metamorphoses into the image of the swine of Eubuleus—the swine that are swallowed up into the earth when Hades carries Persephone down to be the queen of the dead. And a variant of this image occurs in Quentin's last internal monologue before he drowns himself when he imagines the clump of cedars where Candace used to meet her lovers: "Just by imagining the clump it seemed to me that I could hear whispers secret surges smell the beating of hot blood under wild unsecret flesh watching against red eyelids the swine untethered in pairs rushing coupled into the sea."

Since Quentin's incestuous desire for his sister is synonymous with death, it is no surprise that in the scene by the branch, where Quentin puts his knife to his sister's throat and offers to kill her and then himself, their conversation parodies that of sexual intercourse:

> will you close your eyes
> no like this youll have to push it harder
> touch your hand to it . . .
> push it are you going to
> do you want me to
> yes push it
> touch your hand to it

It is a mark of the brilliance and centrality of this scene that its imagery evokes as well the reason for that fear which continually unmans Quentin whenever he tries to assume the masculine role. When Quentin puts his knife to his sister's throat, he is placing his knife at the throat of someone who is an image of himself, thereby evoking the threat of castration—the traditional punishment for incest. The brother seducer with the phallic knife at his sister's throat is as well the brother avenger with the castrating knife at the son's penis. The fear of castration fixes Quentin in secondary narcissism, for by making sexual union with a woman synonymous with death, the castration fear prevents the establishment of a love object outside the ego. Quentin's fear of castration is projected onto the figure of his sister, incest with whom would be punished by castration. Thus in her encounters with Quentin, Candace becomes the castrator. When Candace tells him to go ahead and use the knife, his fear unmans him; he drops the phallic knife and loses it, and when he tells Candace that he will find it in a moment, she asks, "Are you afraid to?" Recall as well that in the scene at the hog wallow Candace says that she tried to scratch Quentin's eyes out. Having failed in the masculine role of brother seducer in relation to Candace, Quentin shifts to a passive, feminine role, and Candace assumes the active, masculine role. It is a shift like the one Quentin undergoes when he fails in the masculine role of brother-avenger in relation to the seducer Dalton Ames; Quentin immediately assumes a feminine role, fainting like a girl in Ames's grasp. Indeed, brooding on that fear of risking his life that caused him to reject Ames's offer of the phallic pistol, Quentin thinks, "And when he put Dalton Ames. Dalton Ames. Dalton Ames. When he put the pistol in my hand I didn't. . . . Dalton Ames. Dalton Ames. Dalton Ames. If I could have been his mother lying with open body lifted laughing, holding his father with my hand refraining, seeing, watching him die before he lived."

The explanation for this shifting from a masculine to a feminine role is to be found in the son's ambivalence toward his father in the castration complex. On the one hand, there is an aggressive reaction of the son toward the castrating father, a desire for the father's death, a desire to kill him. But on the other hand, there is a tender reaction, a desire to renounce the object that has caused the father's anger, to give up the penis and thus retain the father's love by assuming a passive, feminine role in relation to him—in short, to become the mother in relation to the father. In this situation (the tender, passive reaction) the fear of castration turns into a longing for castration, and since, as Freud points out, the fear of death is an analogue of the fear of castration, this transformation of the castration fear into a desire for castration within the incest scenario has as its analogue, within the scenario of narcissistic doubling, that fear of death that becomes a longing for death—the paradox, as Rank says, of a thanatophobia that leads to suicide. What the fear of castration is to incest the fear of death is to doubling, and as the fear of castration and the fear of death are analogues, so too are incest and doubling. We need only recall in this connection that the characteristic doubling scenario of madness leading to suicide is simply a partial form of self-destruction. During the walk in the country that Quentin takes on the day of his suicide, he stops on a bridge and looks down at his shadow in the water and remembers,

> Versh told me about a man mutilated himself. He went into the woods and did it with a razor, sitting in a ditch. A broken razor flinging them backward over his shoulder the same motion complete the jerked skein of blood backward not looping. But that's not it. It's not having them. It's never to have had them then I could say O That That's Chinese I don't know Chinese. And Father said it's because you are a virgin: dont you see? Women are never virgins. Purity is a negative state and therefore contrary to nature. It's nature is hurting you not Caddy and I said That's just words and he said So is virginity and I said you dont know. You cant know and he said Yes. On the instant when we come to realise that tragedy is second-hand.
>
> Where the shadow of the bridge fell I could see down for a long way, but not as far as the bottom.

In a real or imagined conversation with his father, bits of which recur during his internal narrative, Quentin confesses that he and Candace have committed incest, and he seeks a punishment, he says, that will isolate himself and his sister from the loud world. When his father asks him if he tried to force Candace to commit incest, Quentin replies, "i was afraid to i was afraid she might." It is as if in seeking to be punished for incest, to be castrated, Quentin would have proof that his masculinity had ever been potent enough to constitute a threat to the father; castration would constitute the father's acknowledgment of the son's manhood. . . .

When Quentin demands that his father act against the seducer Dalton Ames, Quentin, by taking this initiative, is in effect trying to supplant his father, to seize his authority. But Quentin's father refuses to act, and the sense of Mr. Compson's refusal is that Quentin cannot seize his father's authority because there is no authority to seize. Quentin's alcoholic, nihilistic father presents himself as an emasculated son, ruined by General Compson's failure. Mr. Compson psychologically castrates Quentin by confronting him with a father figure, a model for manhood, who is himself a castrated son. Mr. Compson possesses no authority that Quentin could seize because what Mr. Compson inherited from the General was not power but impotence. If Quentin is a son struggling in the grip of Father Time, so is his father. And it is exactly that argument that Mr. Compson uses against Quentin. When Quentin demands that they act against the seducer, Mr. Compson answers in essence, "Do you realize how many times this has happened before and how many times it will happen again? You are seeking a once-and-for-all solution to this problem, but there are no once-and-for-all solutions. One has no force, no authority to act in this matter because one has no originality. The very repetitive nature of time precludes the existence of originality within its cycles. You cannot be the father because I am not the father—only Time is the father." When Quentin demands that they avenge Candace's virginity, his father replies, "Women are never virgins. Purity is a negative state and therefore contrary to nature. It's nature hurting you not Caddy and I said That's just words and he said So is virginity and I said you dont know. You cant know and he said Yes. On the instant when we come to realise that tragedy is second-hand." In essence Quentin's father says, "We cannot act because there exists no virginity to avenge and because there exists no authority by which we could avenge since we have no originality. We are second-hand. You are a copy of a copy. To you, a son who has only been a son, it might seem that a father has authority because he comes first, but to one who has been both a father and a son, it is clear that to come before is not necessarily to come first, that priority is not necessarily originality. My fate was determined by my father as your fate is determined by yours." Quentin's attempt to avenge his sister's lost virginity (proving thereby that it had once existed) and maintain the family honor is an attempt to maintain the possibility of "virginity" in a larger sense, the possibility of the existence of a virgin space within which one can still be first, within which one can have authority through originality, a virgin space like that Mississippi wilderness into which the first Compson (Jason Lycurgus I) rode in 1811 to seize the land later known as the Compson Domain, the land "fit to breed princes, statesmen and generals and bishops, to avenge the dispossessed Compsons from Culloden and Carolina and Kentucky," just as Sutpen came to Mississippi to get land and found a dynasty that would avenge the dispossessed Sutpens of West Virginia. In a letter to Malcolm Cowley, Faulkner said that Quentin regarded Sutpen as "originless." Which is to say, that being without origin, Sutpen tries to become his own origin, his own father, an attempt implicit in the very act of choosing a father figure to replace his real father. When Quentin tells the story of the Sutpens in *Absalom*, he is not just telling his own personal story, he is telling the story of the Compson family as well.

The event that destroyed Sutpen's attempt to found a dynasty is the same event that began the decline of the Compson family—the Civil War closed off the virgin space and the time of origins, so that the antebellum South became in the minds of postwar Southerners that debilitating "golden age and lost world" in comparison with which the present is inadequate. The decline of the Compsons began with General Compson "who failed at Shiloh in '62 and failed again though not so badly at Resaca in '64, who put the first mortgage on the still intact square mile to a New England carpetbagger in '66, after the old town had been burned by the Federal General Smith and the new little town, in time to be populated mainly by the descendants not of Compsons but of Snopeses, had begun to encroach and then nibble at and into it as the failed brigadier spent the next forty years selling fragments of it off to keep up the mortgage on the remainder." The last of the Compson Domain is sold by Quentin's father to send Quentin to Harvard.

Mr. Compson's denial of the existence of an authority by which he could act necessarily entails his denial of virginity, for there is no possibility of that originality from which authority springs if there is no virgin space within which one can be first. And for the same reason Quentin's obsession with Candace's loss of virginity is necessarily an obsession with his own impotence, since the absence of the virgin space renders him powerless. When Mr. Compson refuses to act against Dalton Ames, Quentin tries to force him to take some action by claiming that he and Candace have committed incest—that primal affront to the authority of the father. But where there is no authority there can be no affront, and where the father feels his own inherited impotence, he cannot believe that his son has power. Mr. Compson tells Quentin that he doesn't believe that he and Candace committed incest, and Quentin says, "If we could have just done something so dreadful and Father said That's sad too, people cannot do anything that dreadful they cannot do anything very dreadful at all they cannot even remember tomorrow what seemed dreadful today and I said, You can shirk all things and he said, Ah can you." Since Mr. Compson believes that man is helpless in the grip of time, that everything is fated, there is no question of shirking or not shirking, for there is no question of willing. In discussing the revenge against time, Nietzsche speaks of those preachers of despair who say, "Alas the stone *It was* cannot be moved," and Mr. Compson's last words in Quentin's narrative are "was the saddest word of all there is nothing else in the world its not despair until time its not even time until it was."

Is there no virgin space in which one can be first, in which one can have authority through originality? This is the question that Quentin must face in trying to decide whether his father is right, whether he is doomed to be an impotent failure like his father and grandfather. And it is in light of this question that we can gain an insight into Quentin's act of narration in *Absalom*, for what is at work in Quentin's struggle to bring the story of the Sutpens under control is the question of whether narration itself constitutes a space in which one can be original, whether an "author" possesses "authority," whether that repetition which in life Quentin has experienced as a compulsive fate can be transformed in narration, through an act of the will, into a power, a mastery of time.

The Sound and the Fury
and the Dislocation of Form

Donald M. Kartiganer

The Sound and the Fury is the four-times-told tale that opens with a date and the disorder of an idiot's mind and concludes with "post and tree, window and doorway, and signboard, each in its ordered place." But this final order is one that has meaning only for the idiot: a sequence of objects that, when viewed from one perspective rather than another, can calm Benjy into a serene silence. The reader remains in a welter of contradictory visions.

None of the four tales speaks to another, each imagined order cancels out the one that precedes it. Truth is the meaningless sum of four items that seem to have no business being added: Benjy plus Quentin plus Jason plus the "narrator." " 'You bring them together,' " as Faulkner wrote in *Absalom, Absalom!*, " '. . . and . . . nothing happens.' " This atomized Southern family, caught in the conflicts of ancient honor, modern commercialism, self-pity, cynicism, diseased love, becomes Faulkner's impassioned metaphor for the modern crisis of meaning. And *The Sound and the Fury* becomes, paradoxically, a vital expression of the failure of imagination, an approximation of what, for Frank Kermode, is no novel at all: "a discontinuous unorganized middle" that lacks the beginning and end of novel-time (*The Sense of an Ending*).

Neither in the figure of Caddy, for some an organizing center of the novel, nor in the well-wrought fourth narrative do we find an adequate basis of unity in the work. The former possibility has been encouraged in several places by Faulkner himself, who claimed that the story began with the image of Caddy in the tree, and that she is its center, "what I wrote the book about." But rather than a means of binding the fragments together, the image is itself complicated by the fragmentation. It moves into that isolation within the memory, eternal and not quite relevant, that all the major images of the novel possess. Millgate reveals a common uneasiness about this problem: "The novel revolves upon Caddy, but Caddy herself escapes satisfactory definition." The accumulation of monologues results in neither a unity of vision nor a unity of envisioners.

The Benjy section represents extreme objectivity, a condition impossible to the ordinary mind and far in excess of even the most naturalistic fiction. In their sections Quentin and Jason are extremely subjective, each imposing a distorted view on experience, in exact contrast to Benjy, who can abstract no order at all. The fourth section is the voice of the traditional novelist, combining in moderation the qualities of the first three sections: objective in that it seems to tell us faithfully and credibly what happens (our faith in Quentin and Jason is, of course, minimal), and at the same time interpretive but without obvious distortion. Following upon the total immersion in experience or self of the three brothers, the last section is told entirely from without, and establishes the kind of comprehensive but still fixed clarity we expect to find in fiction. And yet for those very qualities, which for many are its strengths, it does not—even as the others do not— tell us what we most need to know.

The Benjy section comes first in the novel for the simple reason that Benjy, of all the narrators, cannot lie, which is to say he cannot create. Being an idiot, Benjy is perception prior to consciousness, prior to the human need to abstract from events an intelligible order. His monologue is a series of frozen pictures, offered without bias: "Through the fence, between the curling flower spaces, I could see them hitting"; " 'What do you want' Jason said. He had his hands in his pockets and a pencil behind his ear"; "[Father] drank and set the glass down and went and put his hand on Mother's shoulder." His metaphors have the status of fact: "Caddy smelled like trees."

The quality of Benjy's memory is the chief indicator of his nonhuman perception, for he does not recollect the past: he relives it.

> "Wait a minute." Luster said. "You snagged on that nail again. Cant you never crawl through here without snagging on that nail."
>
> *Caddy uncaught me and we crawled through. Uncle Maury said to not let anybody see us, so we better stoop over, Caddy said. Stoop over, Benjy. Like this, see. We stooped over and crossed the garden,*

where the flowers rasped and rattled against us. The ground was hard.
We climbed the fence, where the pigs were grunting and snuffing. I
expect they're sorry because one of them got killed today, Caddy said.
The ground was hard, churned and knotted.

Keep your hands in your pockets, Caddy said. Or they'll get froze.
You don't want your hands froze on Christmas, do you.

"It's too cold out there." Versh said. "You dont want to go
out doors."

The sequence begins in the present, April 7, 1928, with Benjy and
Luster crawling through a fence to get to the branch, where Luster hopes
to find a golf ball. It shifts to a winter day of Benjy's childhood, when he
and Caddy are also crawling through a fence on their way to deliver a note
from Uncle Maury to Mrs. Patterson. The scene shifts again to earlier the
same day, before Caddy has come home from school.

These shifts are triggered by a nail, a fence, the coldness—some object
or quality that abruptly springs Benjy into a different time zone, each one
of which is as alive and real for Benjy as the present. Strictly speaking he
"remembers" nothing. As Faulkner said of Benjy in 1955, "To that idiot,
time was not a continuation, it was an instant, there was no yesterday and
no tomorrow, it all is this moment, it all is (now) to him. He cannot
distinguish between what was last year and what will be tomorrow, he
doesn't know whether he dreamed it, or saw it."

Time as duration—Bergsonian time—is what Faulkner is alluding to
here; and it is this sense of time that Benjy, by virtue of his idiocy, has
abandoned. Memory does not serve him as it serves the normal mind,
becoming part of the mind and integral to the stream of constantly created
perception that makes it up: the past which, as Bergson put it, "gnaws into
the future and which swells as it advances" (*Creative Evolution*, trans. Arthur
Mitchell). Benjy does not recall, and therefore cannot interpret, the past
from the perspective of the present; nor does the past help to determine
that perspective. Instead of past and present being a continuum, each in-
fluencing the meaning of the other, they have no temporal dimension at
all. They are isolated, autonomous moments that do not come "before" or
"after."

This freedom from time makes Benjy a unique narrator indeed. He
does not perceive reality but is at one with it; he does not need to create
life but rather possesses it with a striking immediacy. There is a timelessness
in the scenes Benjy relives, but it is not the timelessness of art, abstracting
time into meaning. It is the absence of the need for art.

Benjy's monologue, then, does not constitute an interpretation at all; what he tells us is life, not text. Emerging as if from the vantage point of eternal stasis, where each moment lived (whether for the first or fiftieth time) is the original moment and the only moment, unaffected by any of the others, this telling is an affront to the existence of narration or of novels. As Bleikasten says, it "is the very negation of narrative." This is one of the reasons why the Benjy section has such a hold on us, why we attribute to it an authority we never think of granting the others, especially the narratives of his two brothers. Spoken with the awareness that time is always present, and thus missing that sense of consecutiveness necessary to our quick understanding, Benjy's monologue is difficult; yet the cause of that difficulty persuades us that this is truth, not art.

The irony, however, and the reason why the novel does not simply end with this section, is that while Benjy is not himself formulating an interpretation, his succession of lived images passes over into *our* interpretation, becomes a temporal fiction of Compson history that is so clear it is unbelievable. Benjy's scenes, despite fractured chronology and abrupt transitions, meld into a set of clear and consistent character portraits—two-dimensional figures with the sharpness of allegorical signposts that elicit from us simplistic evaluations empty of deep moral insight. "But for the very reason of their simplicity," one critic has written, "Benjy's responses function as a quick moral index to events"(John W. Hunt, *William Faulkner: Art in Theological Tension*). This is indeed the effect of Benjy's monologue and its danger.

The following passage, taken from the end of Benjy's monologue, is typical. This is the night of Damuddy's death, when Quentin, Caddy, Jason, and Benjy (between the ages of three and eight) are being put to bed:

> There were two beds. Quentin got in the other one. He turned his face to the wall. Dilsey put Jason in with him. Caddy took her dress off.
>
> "Just look at your drawers." Dilsey said. "You better be glad your ma aint seen you."
>
> "I already told on her." Jason said.
>
> "I bound you would." Dilsey said.
>
> "And see what you got by it." Caddy said. "Tattletale."
>
> "What did I get by it." Jason said.
>
> "Whyn't you get your nightie on." Dilsey said. She went and helped Caddy take off her bodice and drawers. "Just look at you." Dilsey said. She wadded the drawers and scrubbed Caddy

behind with them. "It done soaked clean through onto you." she said. "But you wont get no bath this night. Here." She put Caddy's nightie on her and Caddy climbed into the bed and Dilsey went to the door and stood with her hand on the light. "You all be quiet now, you hear." she said.

"All right." Caddy said. "Mother's not coming in tonight." she said. "So we still have to mind me."

"Yes." Dilsey said. "Go to sleep, now."

"Mother's sick." Caddy said. "She and Damuddy are both sick."

"Hush." Dilsey said. "You go to sleep."

The room went black, except the door. Then the door went black. Caddy said, "Hush, Maury," putting her hand on me. So I stayed hushed. We could hear us. We could hear the dark.

It went away, and Father looked at us. He looked at Quentin and Jason, then he came and kissed Caddy and put his hand on my head.

"Is Mother very sick." Caddy said.

"No." Father said. "Are you going to take good care of Maury."

"Yes." Caddy said.

Within the space of a single, short scene, each member of the Compson household is definitively characterized. Quentin is the figure of impotence, the one who turns his face to the wall, expressing his futile outrage at all that has gone on that day. Jason, meanness personified, has already told on Caddy—without particular benefit, although he does not realize this. Dilsey is the loyal retainer, the embodiment of responsible affection, who undresses and cleans up Caddy and sees to it that all the children are in bed. Mother's lack of responsibility is defined by her absence: she is "sick." Father makes his appearance, to look at Jason and Quentin, and to kiss Caddy and touch Benjy (still named Maury): *almost* the responsible parent but playing his favorites and, in his last words, delegating responsibility for Benjy to Caddy. Caddy herself is love, the one who can quiet Benjy down with the touch of her hand. She is also the boldness of youth as both her dirty underwear and confident assumption of the mother's role indicate.

What is so striking about this scene is not only that the meaning of each character can be summarized in an abstract word or two, but that, although the scene comes at the end of Benjy's monologue, the characters are the same as they were in the beginning. They exhibit little change or development; nor can Benjy develop significantly his understanding of them. Each character must be himself over and over again, bearing, like a gift of birth, his inescapable moral worth.

Life—for the scenes Benjy witnesses are at one level the most authentic in the novel—retains the power of its rawness, its freedom from structure; yet simultaneously it passes into the order of our interpretation: a coherent fiction implying all-too-clear moral attitudes. And the demands of our own reader's role are such that it is impossible for us to reverse the process, to return this charged but implausible text to its state of pure presence in the mind of the nonnarrator where it originates.

The most difficult task in reading *The Sound and the Fury* is to get beyond this opening section, for finally Benjy is demonstrating the poverty of the pure witness of what is unquestionably there. Benjy's monologue is never less, or more, than truth. We must pass on to the next three sections in which this truth confronts deliberate distortion: vested interests organizing, plotting—consciously or unconsciously, violently or subtly. And with these distortions the cautionary fable we have gleaned from Benjy's images collapses into new complexities: Caddy's promises succumb to need, Jason's ruthlessness turns over into psychotic paranoia, Quentin's futility rages in dreams of murder and incest.

Yet the collapse is not total, as much of the criticism of the novel attests. Not the least irony of *The Sound and the Fury* is that we are tempted most by an absolutism that the whole structure of the novel teaches us to dismiss: not because it is not true but because it is not the truth of what it means to be human in that world which, so this novel asserts, is the one that exists.

Following Benjy's freedom from time and interpretation comes the time-possessed Quentin, who wants nothing more than to *replace* life with interpretation. Reality for Quentin is primarily change—in particular the change implicit to the sexual identity of his sister Caddy—and interpretation, metaphor, is the created ground of permanence in which change is eliminated. Caddy's development from child to adolescent and her subsequent loss of virginity epitomizes that change which, in Quentin's mind, is the essence of confusion.

> Until after the honeysuckle got all mixed up in it the whole thing came to symbolise night and unrest I seemed to be lying neither asleep nor awake looking down a long corridor of grey halflight where all stable things had become shadowy paradoxical all I had done shadows all I had felt suffered taking visible form

antic and perverse mocking without relevance inherent themselves with the denial of the significance they should have affirmed thinking I was I was not who was not was not who.

Against this vision of formlessness Quentin props a Byronic fable of incest between himself and Caddy, thus guiding what Father calls her "natural human folly" into a horrific one. Through metaphor he informs his confusion with the clarity of hell: *"the pointing and the horror walled by the clean flame."* But what is most important is that this hell, and the incest that enables Quentin and Caddy to deserve it, is purely imaginary. In the crucial interview that brings Quentin's monologue to a close, Father asks him: "did you try to make her do it and i i was afraid to i was afraid she might and then it wouldnt have done any good but if i could tell you we did it would have been so and then the others wouldnt be so and then the world would roar away."

"If i could tell you we did it would have been so." It is not an actual hell reserved for actual sinners that Quentin wants, but his invented one whose unreality frees it from a confusing and disappointing world. Purity for Quentin lies in a fiction, *known* as a fiction and priding itself on its indifference to reality. He is trying to transform life from within its midst, to convert dull promiscuity to sin, his dreary frustrations into a hell of rich and well-defined despair. It is a hell necessarily unreal: actual incest with Caddy "wouldnt have done any good."

Confronted everywhere with his impotence, Quentin is desperate to believe in the power of words alone: to substitute for what-is the names of what-is-not. He wants to convince Caddy of the reality of his fantasy, not that they have literally made love but that words have a substance more real than bodies.

> *I'll tell you how it was it was a crime we did a terrible crime it cannot be hid you think it can but wait   Poor Quentin youve never done that have you   and I'll tell you how it was I'll tell Father then itll have to be because you love Father then we'll have to go away amid the pointing and the horror the clean flame I'll make you say we did I'm stronger than you I'll make you know we did you thought it was them but it was me listen I fooled you all the time it was me.*

Quentin tries to get Caddy to accede to this fantasy, to see words as the originator rather than the imitator of deeds. This is Quentin's willful decadence, a version of his subsequent suicide in that it puts the world away, using a metaphor as a wedge between language and life. As Mr.

Compson says, Quentin is trying to make "a temporary state of mind . . . symmetrical above the flesh." In this sense he is like the three young boys in Cambridge talking about what they might do with the prize money for a fish they neither have caught nor have any hope of catching: "They all talked at once, their voices insistent and contradictory and impatient, making of unreality a possibility, then a probability, then an incontrovertible fact, as people will when their desires become words."

Quentin's need to alter an unbearable reality through language owes much to the teachings of his father. On the first page of Quentin's monologue we read: "Because no battle is ever won he said. They are not even fought. The field only reveals to man his own folly and despair, and victory is an illusion of philosophers and fools." And shortly before the end: "Father was teaching us that all men are just accumulations dolls stuffed with sawdust swept up from the trash heaps where all previous dolls had been thrown away." Mr. Compson's theme has been the futility of human action.

Anxious to believe his father is wrong, Quentin clings to the moral codes of Southern antebellum myth: if a woman has been deflowered it can only be because "he made you do it let him he was stronger than you," and a loyal brother will avenge her: "tomorrow Ill kill him I swear I will." But finally this melodramatic interpretation of events will not do, and so Quentin escapes the cynicism of his father by embracing fully the idea of impotence: the pure fantasy of incest that signals the abandonment of time and his entrance into a world of words.

Quentin's behavior on June 2, 1910, parallels his quest for an irrelevant language. He moves toward a stylization of his life by separating his deeds from his purposes, the conduct of his last day from the impact of its destination. Cutting his thumb on his broken watch crystal, Quentin administers iodine in order to prevent infection; he attends to the matter of packing his belongings, writing farewell notes, stacking books, like someone going on vacation or moving to another town. At the end he carefully removes a blood stain from his vest, washes, cleans his teeth, and brushes his hat, before leaving his room to drown himself.

Both forms of metaphor, verbal and behavioral, move toward suicide. Driving words further and further from facts, style from purpose, art from meaning, Quentin is inside death—the place without life—for much of his monologue. And yet, since the pride of his fiction-making is its admitted distance from the real, Quentin cannot help but acknowledge the agony of what is: that he has not committed incest with Caddy, that she has several lovers, that she is pregnant with one man's child and is married to another, a "blackguard." There is in all this an affont that Quentin's artistry cannot conceal or bear. His only triumph is that he has proved his father wrong at least about one thing: "no man ever does that [commits Suicide] under the first fury of despair or remorse or bereavement."

The deliberate flight from fact that dominates Quentin's monologue reverses the effect of Benjy's monologue that precedes it. Benjy has made us aware of the distortion of the *literal;* his language is exact, free of bias. It is truth, not metaphor. Yet this exaggerated objectivism results in the most simplistic of moral designs. Quentin, on the other hand, has plunged into metaphor; but in doing so he reduces subjectivism to an art of decadence: "symmetrical above the flesh."

"The first sane Compson since before Culloden," Faulkner said of Jason in the Appendix to *The Sound and the Fury* written sixteen years after the novel. This is a view that has been adopted wholly or in part by many readers of the novel, although one wonders how anyone, especially Faulkner, could have considered Jason sane or rational. Surely Jason is as removed from what we generally consider sanity as any character in *The Sound and the Fury.* He is in fact far less aware of what is actually real than his brother Quentin. Such is our quickness in the twentieth century to polarize rationality and emotion, intellectual and intuitive responses, that critical interpretation of *The Sound and the Fury* has found it easy to set Jason up as its rational villain, the opposite number of the high-minded, intuitive Sartorises and Compsons, and probably, with white-trash Snopeses and invading Yankees, the secret of the fall of man in the Faulkner world. Such a thesis is hardly adequate for the kind of complexity Faulkner offers us here and elsewhere in his fiction. Faulkner may indeed be on the side of intuition, particularly as Bergson described it, but in his best work he does not demonstrate that preference by neat categories of the kind in which Jason has been pigeon-holed.

A man who says, "I wouldn't bet on any team that fellow Ruth played on. . . . Even if I knew it was going to win"—to pick out only one example—is hardly the epitome of cold-hearted business-like behavior. And that he could ever have "competed with and held his own with the Snopeses," as Faulkner writes in the Appendix, is incredible. No man who is fooled and humiliated so many times in one day by everyone from Miss Quentin to Old Man Job, is going to be a match for Flem Snopes, whose coldly analytic inhumanity has so often been wrongly identified with Jason. The latter's insistence that he would not bet on a sure winner is not only irrational, it is even the mark of a curious idealism. It is also a significant, usually ignored, side of this pathetic man who spends his Good Friday crucifying himself on the crosses he alone provides.

A psychotic, some wit once said, is a man who honestly believes that two plus two equals five; a neurotic knows very well that two plus two equals four—but it bothers him. Let this be our hint as to the difference between Jason and Quentin, for Quentin deliberately composes an incest fable in order to deal with a reality he cannot face. That it *is* a fable is something he himself insists on. Jason, however, confuses the real and the illusory, and is quite unaware of the way he arranges his own punishment. Standing between him and reality is his need to hold on to two opposing views of himself: one is that he is completely sufficient, the other is that he is the scrapegoat of the world. On one hand Jason considers himself an effective operator, family head, market speculator, brainy swindler of Caddy and her daughter, a man of keen business sense. On the other hand he nurtures the dream of his victimization, his suffering at the hands of the Compsons, the Gibsons, his boss Earl, even the telegraph company.

Jason's entire monologue wanders through a maze of contradiction that cannot be reduced to mere hypocrisy or rationalization. With $7,000 stashed away, the accumulation of fifteen years of theft, Jason thinks "money has no value; it's just the way you spend it. It dont belong to anybody, so why try to hoard it." Regretting that he must be a detective, he yet makes the pursuit of his niece Quentin a major project. Insisting only that she show "discretion," fearing that someday he'll find her "under a wagon on the square," he nevertheless chases her far out into the country on a day when nearly everyone else is at the traveling show in town, when there is no one else to see her but himself. He scoffs at Compson pride in blood, yet later it is his and his mother's name that Quentin is making "a byword in the town." He firmly believes that it is Caddy who has deceived *him,* who has broken her promises to him, and that Quentin, in letting the air out of his tires, has given back far more than she received: "I just wouldn't do you this way. I wouldn't do you this way no matter what you had done to me." And in the midst of all this double-dealing and plain fraud, Jason can sincerely say, "If there's one thing gets under my skin, it's a damn hypocrite."

Within this web of opposed purposes—is it comfort or suffering that he seeks?—Jason seems absent of any objective awareness of those realities most relevant to him. He is confusion incarnate, guilty of all he seems to hate, hating his own image in others, the least sane and the most perversely imaginative of all the Compsons. When the world threatens him with satisfaction, when his niece heeds his insistence on discretion by driving with her man friend into an abandoned countryside, Jason chases after her, contradicting his own wishes so that his pain can be adequate to his unintelligible need. Quentin creates in order to avoid suffering, Jason, to experience it.

Surely we cannot match criteria of sanity or cold logic with what goes on in Jason's mind on April 6, 1928. For Bergson, the analytic mind is capable of the "ingenious arrangement of immobilities" (*A Study in Metaphysics: The Creative Mind,* trans. Mabelle L. Andison). It is the kind of perception that orders reality rather than entering into sympathetic union with it. But Jason's organization of things is so confused and contradictory that we can hardly observe in him the sense of conscious control that Bergson identifies with the analytic mind. Jason's most obvious quality, visible in all his pratfalls, is his inability to *utilize* reality, to make it integral to a specific design. To compare him with Faulkner's master of analytic reasoning, Flem Snopes, is to see how absurdly distant he is from Flem.

The meanness with which Jason confronts the world is the cover that scarcely conceals his lack of self-knowledge. His agony is real, but he cannot begin to explain its source or its meaning. The only language he can risk is the stream of impotent insult he inflicts on everything around him. The result, after the pathos of Benjy and the occasionally burdensome rhetorical self-indulgence of Quentin, is some uproarious invective: "I haven't got much pride, I can't afford it with a kitchen full of niggers to feed and robbing the state asylum of its star freshman. Blood, I says, governors and generals. It's a damn good thing we never had any kings and presidents; we'd all be down there at Jackson chasing butterflies." Following Benjy and Quentin, this sort of thing comes as bracing, if low, comedy. And it reminds us, even in this grim study of family disintegration, of the variety of Faulkner's voices and his daring willingness to use them.

Thus Faulkner adds still one more piece to his exploration of the possibilities of vision. Still subjective, as opposed to the more objective first and fourth sections, but substantially different from Quentin's, Jason's is the mind that seems to have dissolved the boundaries of fact and invention, not as they might be dissolved in the collaboration within a supreme fiction, but as in the furthest stages of paranoia. The great irony of the section is that Jason is the one Compson who creates the appearance of ordinary social existence: he holds a job, wears a hat, visits a whorehouse regularly, and manages to fool his mother into burning what she believes are Caddy's checks. But his existence is actually a chaos of confused motion, utter disorder within the mind. Quentin, preparing methodically for suicide, is a study in contrast.

With "April Eighth 1928" the novel moves outward, away from the sealed monologues of Benjy, Quentin, and Jason. The telling of the Compson history from within passes to the telling from without. It is the last possibility Faulkner must exhaust in order to make his wasteland of sensibility complete; the traditional fictional method of the removed narrator describing objectively the characters and the events and, without a sense of excessive intrusion, interpreting them for us.

For the first time in the book we get novelistic description: weather, place, persons, the appearance of things from the eye of a detached but interested spectator: "The day dawned bleak and chill, a moving wall of grey light out of the northeast which, instead of dissolving into moisture, seemed to disintegrate into minute and venomous particles, like dust that, when Dilsey opened the door of the cabin and emerged, needled laterally into her flesh, precipitating not so much a moisture as a substance partaking of the quality of thin, not quite congealed oil." And with this description a new voice enters the novel: "She had been a big woman once but now her skeleton rose, draped loosely in unpadded skin that tightened again upon a paunch almost dropsical, as though muscle and tissue had been courage or fortitude which the days or the years had consumed until only the indomitable skelton was left rising like a ruin or a landmark above the somnolent and impervious guts." It is a rhetorical voice, set apart from the chaos and the distortion we have already seen. And from its secure perch, intimate with the events yet aloof from the pain of being a Compson, this voice seeks to tell us the meaning of what has come before.

Benjy, so brilliantly rendered in his own voice in the first section, is now described from the outside.

> Luster entered, followed by a big man who appeared to have been shaped of some substance whose particles would not or did not cohere to one another or to the frame which supported it. His skin was dead looking and hairless; dropsical too, he moved with a shambling gait like a trained bear. His hair was pale and fine. It had been brushed smoothly down upon his brow like that of children in daguerrotypes. His eyes were clear, of the pale sweet blue of cornflowers, his thick mouth hung open, drooling a little.

One is almost shocked by the description—is this Benjy? Having wrestled with the process of his mind, we find this external view like the portrait of someone else, another idiot from another novel. Not only described, he is also interpreted: "Then Ben wailed again, hopeless and prolonged. It was nothing. Just sound. It might have been all time and injustice and sorrow become vocal for an instant by a conjunction of planets."

Jason, once again in pursuit of Quentin, this time for the $7,000 she has taken from his room, is also described "with close-thatched brown hair curled into two stubborn hooks, one on either side of his forehead like a bartender in caricature," and his meaning is wrested from the confusion of his own monologue. The narrator focuses chiefly on the bank job promised Jason years ago, which he never received because of Caddy's divorce from Herbert. It is supposedly neither Quentin nor the money he is really chasing: "they merely symbolized the job in the bank of which he had been deprived before he ever got it." What has been stolen from him this time is simply "that which was to have compensated him for the lost job, which he had acquired through so much effort and risk, by the very symbol of the lost job itself."

With both Benjy and Jason a great deal has been lost in the abstraction of meaning from movement. From the total immersion of the private monologue we move to the detached external view; from confused and confusing versions of reality we get an orderly, consistent portrait of the Compson family. And yet this clarity does not explain; these interpretations of Jason and Benjy seem pale and inadequate beside their respective monologues. Can Jason's terible confusion, for example, really be embraced by the motive attributed to him in this section? There is a curious irrelevance here, as if in this achieved meaning one were reading about different characters entirely. And yet in the earlier monologues we have already seen the inadequacies of personal distortion and the two-dimensional clarity of pure perception.

My point here is not simply a determined refusal to admit the comprehensiveness of what I am reading. It is rather to recognize that in this fourth attempt to tell the Compson story we are still faced with the problems of the first three, namely, a failure of the creation of a sufficient form. And this failure becomes itself the form, and therefore the meaning, of *The Sound and the Fury*. The four fragments, each a fully achieved expression of voice operating within the severest limitations, remain separate and incoherent.

The fourth section is, of course, the easiest to read. It is divided into four parts: the scene in the house Easter morning, showing Dilsey at work and the discovery of the stolen money; the Easter service at church; Jason's pursuit of Quentin; and the short scene in which Luster tries to take Benjy to the graveyard through town. The polarities of Dilsey's and the Compson's existence are emphatic, especially in the juxtaposition of the Easter service, in its celebration of God's time, and Jason's mad chase, his striving in the context of human time. Dilsey, understanding the broken clock in the kitchen or the "beginning and the ending" in church, has a sure grasp of both.

Dilsey has been pointed to as the one source of value in the novel, supported by the comment in what seems to me an invariably misleading appendix, and it is clear that she embodies much that the Compsons lack, especially a sense of duty to her position as servant and her total faith in God. It is also clear that her service to the family has not been enough to save it, and that even her own children disobey her often, in certain instances emulating the Compson sin of pride. Her religious faith is remote as far as the Compsons are concerned. If the Christian myth is being put forth here as a source of order in the world, it clearly has only ironic reference to them.

> "I know you blame me," Mrs. Compson said, "for letting
> them off to go to church today."
> "Go where?" Jason said. "Hasn't that damn show left yet?"

But Dilsey is irrelevant not only to the Compsons but to those assumptions of the nature of reality basic to the novel. Unlike the other members of the Compson household, and unlike the perspective implicit to this fragmented novel, Dilsey possesses a "mythic" view of the world, the assurance of an enduring order that presides over human existence, organizing it into an intelligible history. It is an order she has not invented but inherited, a traditional Christianity providing meaning and direction to her life. Outside the dissonance and distortion of the first three narratives, the grotesque visions we can never dismiss or corroborate, Dilsey's orthodoxy is a controlled and clear point of view—yet it is remote from that complexity of existence by which the novel lives.

Dilsey transcends chaos by her vision of Christian order.

> "I've seed de first en de last," Dilsey said. "Never you mind
> me."
> "First en last whut?" Frony said.
> "Never you mind." Dilsey said. "I seed de beginnin, en now
> I sees de endin."

This is what Quentin wishes he could do: see in the midst of action the direction of action, understand the living moment because it is part of a history that has already, and always, ended. Dilsey has this gift because she is a Christian. She exists not as one whose life unfolds in surprise, each moment a new and frightening Now, but as one who knows every step of the way because there is in fact only one history. The traditional narrative form of this section of The Sound and the Fury rests on similar assumptions.

Its externally placed perspective, its clear plotting, its coherent analysis of what the behavior of Benjy and Jason means—all of these are basic to a fiction that believes in endings and their power to press into service, and thus make intelligible, each single moment. Dilsey is the center of "April Eighth 1928" because she is the spiritual embodiment of the fictional tradition in which it is told.

Dilsey has what Frank Kermode calls a sense of an ending. For her, the deterioration of the Compsons only confirms the demise of the godless and prideful, and brings still nearer the moment toward which all history moves. Yet the whole of *The Sound and the Fury* does not subscribe to the implications of ending, in terms of either the resolution of action into meaning or the reconciliation of fragments into a controlling system. Dilsey's special understanding, as Frony's question makes clear—"First en last whut?"—is unavailable to any of the major characters in the novel. Nor is it available to the reader unless he ignores three-fourths of that novel, which flatly juxtaposes the last section against the three others that are inconsistent with it, and even confronts Dilsey (and the Easter service that articulates her mode of belief) with the spectacle of Jason's frantic chase after Quentin.

Challenging Dilsey's religious vision is the same sense of time in motion, of a reality intractable to any mental construct, that lays bare the distortions of Quentin and Jason and transforms Benjy's timeless perspective, free of distortion, into a frozen imitation of experience. Neither in the Dilsey section, whatever the power of her characterization or sheer attractiveness as a human being, nor anywhere else in the novel do we see demonstrated the ability of the human imagination to render persuasively the order of things. Instead there is the sense of motion without meaning, of voices in separate rooms talking to no one: the sound and fury that fails to signify.

The Sound and the Fury reads like an anthology of fictional forms, each one of which Faulkner tests and finds wanting. The novel insists on the poverty of created meaning, although in doing so it possesses, like *The Waste Land,* a power that for many readers the later works cannot equal. There is Benjy's unmediated vision of pure presence, that makes of art a kind of impertinence. There are the grotesque orderings of Quentin and Jason—one an effete escapism that seeks a reality dictated by the word, the other subjectivism crippled by paranoia. Both are parodies of the possibility that art might illuminate, not merely distort, the real. And there is the conventional nineteenth-century fiction: the orderly telling of a tale that retreats from all those suspicions of language, concept, external point of view, imposed order, that made the modern possible and necessary.

The achievement of the novel is the honesty of its experiment; we take its "failure" seriously because the attempt seems so genuine and desperate. The basic structure of a compilation of voices or discrete stories is one Faulkner returned to again and again, but never with such a candid admission of the limitations of art. Behind the novel is some as yet vague conception of what literature in the twentieth century might be. Acknowledging, insisting on decreation, making real the time prior to prearrangement, *The Sound and the Fury* yet strives for wholeness, an articulation of design: the form not imposed like a myth from the past but the form that is the consequence of contingent being.

Nearly two decades later, Wallace Stevens expressed the hope of an age.

> To discover an order as of
> A season, to discover summer and know it,
>
> To discover winter and know it well, to find,
> Not to impose, not to have reasoned at all,
> Out of nothing to have come on major weather,
>
> It is possible, possible, possible. It must
> Be possible. It must be that in time
> The real will from its crude compoundings come

The impressiveness of *The Sound and the Fury* is that it accepts nothing it cannot earn. It will have only "major weather." And so the novel sits like a stillborn colossus, always on the verge of beginning.

The Sound and the Fury:
The Search for a Narrative Method

Gary Lee Stonum

The completion of *The Sound and the Fury* in 1929 is the most dramatic turning point in Faulkner's career. The book marks the beginning of his artistic maturity and the end of a lengthy double apprenticeship, first as a poet and then as a novelist. Moreover, it inaugurates the artistic method he will continue to use and develop for the next three decades. Faulkner discovers for the first time in the novel a way of selecting, organizing, and representing his literary materials that is fully compatible with the demands of prose narrative. Still *The Sound and the Fury* remains a transitional work in some ways. In spite of its clear superiority over Faulkner's previous writings, it looks back to the poetry and the apprentice fiction just as much as it anticipates the subsequent major novels. Two divergent conceptions of art confront each other in the book. One is the art of the visionary poet, dreaming of a timeless realm of purity and finding his antecedents among the romantic poets. The other is the art of the realistic novel, broadly defined, and its creator is concerned with the fate of such dreams in a concrete historical environment. He finds his antecedents in the classic novelists of the nineteenth century and in the demonstration by such contemporaries as Joyce and Eliot of new possibilities for the objective representation of deeply personal themes.

Our question is how Faulkner moves from one conception to the other. This in turn requires a close examination of the narrative methods sanctioned

From *Faulkner's Career: An Internal Literary History*. © 1979 by Cornell University. Cornell University Press, 1979.

by each, for it is Faulkner's discovery of a suitable method that most immediately gives rise to the new conception of his artistic goals.

The shift epitomized by *The Sound and the Fury*'s double allegiance is accompanied by at least three other large changes in Faulkner's work. Each of these has some claim to be considered the decisive factor in Faulkner's search for a method. The first is a change in his literary materials. Faulkner himself emphasized the importance of this in a 1955 interview, comparing the discovery that his "little postage stamp of native soil was worth writing about" to the opening of a gold mine. The second is a changed appreciation of the novel as a genre. It results not from his discerning a subtle, previously hidden potential in the genre but from committing himself to its most basic and even obvious characteristics, such as a story involving some form of human conflict. The third is an altered understanding of arrested motion. Before 1929, Faulkner usually stressed the result, arrested motion as a static image of transcendence. In *The Sound and the Fury* he stresses the process, the activity of the writer (and the characters) in arresting motion. Among other things, this gives him an artistic principle more readily compatible with the necessarily temporal structure of narrative.

The first of these changes, the invention of Yoknapatawpha County, is obviously crucial to Faulkner's development, but it seems to me less telling than the other two. Faulkner's initial belief, as reported some years later to Malcolm Cowley, was that a novel should deal with entirely imaginary scenes and people. The belief appears to have contributed to the arty, overly contrived depiction of setting and character in Faulkner's first novel. Certainly, the use of familiar, local materials in the third novel and in the manuscript fragment entitled "Father Abraham" helps Faulkner to avoid such artifice; it also supplies a dense social and historical context of the kind that is sorely lacking in the two earlier novels, *Soldiers' Pay* (1926) and *Mosquitoes* (1927). Both in the 1929 version entitled *Sartoris* and in Douglas Day's reconstruction of the original *Flags in the Dust,* the third novel is actually more diffuse and awkward than its predecessors. Selecting congenial materials is at best only an initial step toward finding a satisfactory means of representing their artistic significance.

In a preface composed for a never-published edition of *The Sound and the Fury,* Faulkner expressly links the advance represented by that book to a new appreciation of its genre. The appreciation is a consequence of writing the book, however, not a prior condition. Only after completing the novel, Faulkner writes in 1933, did he learn how to read—retroactively and without opening a volume—the novelists he had devoured as a youth: Balzac, Conrad, Flaubert, Dostoevsky, and James. Only then did he realize that there was something identifiably and distinctively novelistic "to which the shabby term Art not only can, but must, be applied." The capital letter here is especially revealing, for above all else in the 1920s Faulkner meant his own work to be Art. Moreover, his earliest ideas about what high art should be largely rule out the usual enabling premises of the novel.

In Faulkner's poetry only what escapes the mundane and the quotidian can be truly artistic. Throughout the 1920s Faulkner distinguished the significance of the material world from the fragile symbolic significance that the visionary artist attempted to achieve. The novel, he felt, was obliged to deal primarily with "man in his sorry clay braving chance and circumstance," and so it was fundamentally hostile to visionary methods. "Material and aesthetic significance are not the same, but material importance can destroy artistic importance in spite of what we would like to believe." Thus in the separate reviews of Joseph Hergesheimer's fiction and John Cowper Powys's *Ducdame* from which I have just been quoting, he argues that the overtly poetic and symbolic aspects of their prose had no place in a novel. Nevertheless, his own early novels depend upon precisely what he considered inappropriate in Hergesheimer and Powys. The first three novels (and also the unfinished draft of "Elmer") are not otherwise very like one another in style and theme, but each of them attempts to conform to a visionary conception of Art.

Faulkner's discovery that the novel can have its own kind of artistic significance amounts largely to a belated appropriation of the genre's most ordinary capacities. Indeed, for all that the new method took him several years to find and the rest of his creative life to develop fully, its essential premises are anything but arcane or complicated. Toward the end of his career Faulkner was able to say accurately of his own work that "you write a story to tell about people, man in his constant struggle with his own heart, the hearts of others, or with his environment." The statement, an enlargement upon his assertion in the Nobel Prize speech that a writer's subject ought to be the "human heart in conflict," is an inoffensive enough platitude. The speech has in fact been viewed with dismay by some critics as evidence of Faulkner's inability to understand the daring and complexity of his own best work. The sentiments are remarkable only in that the emphasis on storytelling and on human conflict assumes the method he hadn't yet discovered in the early work.

In order for his materials to constitute a story, the novelist must ordinarily understand them to embody conflicts that do not instantly dissolve into harmony or stalemate. Likewise, according to literary standards that have not changed markedly since Homer, representing the story in a plot entails focusing the conflict by means of such narrative fundamentals as foreshortening, pacing, suspense, and climax. Faulkner's skillful management of such fundamentals has been demonstrated at length by Joseph Reed (*Faulkner's Narrative*). But although this skill is among the glories of Faulkner's mature prose, Reed's argument that Faulkner was first and foremost a storyteller does not hold for the early fiction. In fact, Faulkner's indifference to the need for dramatic conflict was the bane of his otherwise sympathetic editors at *Scribner's Magazine* in the 1920s.

> The trouble with your writing, it seems to me, is that you get mostly the overtones and seem to avoid the real core of the story. It would seem that in the attempt to avoid the obvious you have manufactured the vague. You are skirting around drama and not writing it. It might be worth while to attempt to tell a straightforward tale as you might narrate an incident to a friend, then all this atmosphere and all the background which you sketch in so skillfully will come right handy and make your work distinctive.

The editor assumes, plausibly enough, that he and Faulkner are of one mind about the real core of a story. If they were, the decision to stress drama or to skirt it would be chiefly a question of selecting the locally more effective technique. But Faulkner is practicing an essentially different art in his early fiction, one that in Georg Lukács's terminology is descriptive rather than narrative. As it happens, Lukács disapproved of Faulkner's writing, and he has cited *The Sound and the Fury* as an example of the antirealist modernism he deplored. Yet his distinction corresponds closely to the difference in Faulkner's work before and after 1929. It can help us to specify the important continuities between *The Sound and the Fury* and those nineteenth-century realistic novels that Faulkner has said that writing *The Sound and the Fury* first taught him how to read. Likewise, it can help us to isolate those aspects of the book and of Faulkner's earlier novels that belong to a symbolist art, against which Lukács's ideological objections may be more appropriate.

By the terms narration and description, Lukács refers less to specific literary techniques than to general modes of representation, each implying radically different ideas about the origins of textual meaning. Narrative art determines the meaning of specific elements in the text according to their relation to the concrete situation of the persons represented in the fictional world. "Objects come to life poetically only to the extent that they are related to men's lives; that is why the true epic poet does not describe objects but instead exposes their function in the mesh of human destinies"

("Narrate or Describe"). This functional perspective gives depth and thickness to the fictional world, distributing elements into background or foreground according to their lesser or greater relevance to the represented human lives. Also, it allows that the meaning of objects and events can change as the human situation changes. The perspective is a consequence of narrative art's essential premise, that meaning is immanent in the world. The narrative artist's task is thus to discover and represent the meaning constituted by concrete human situations.

In descriptive art, however, the meaning of an object is no longer ultimately independent of the artistic description. The writer must impose significance on a world that has none of its own or at least none worth writing about. Hence the meaning of any element in the represented world must be measured by its relation to an external, necessarily abstract, and usually static concept. "The loss of the narrative interrelationship between objects and their function in concrete human experience means a loss of artistic significance. Objects can then acquire significance only through direct association with some abstract concept which the author considers essential to his view of the world. But an object does not thereby achieve poetic significance; significance is assigned to it. The object is made a symbol." With respect to the fictional world, this concept is necessarily transcendental, and in visionary art it may well be so with respect to the writer's world also. In either case the concept warrants the meaning of the writer's text and governs his compositional techniques.

Lukács polemically draws the line between these two modes more sharply than can be fully justified. Without his occasionally naive epistemological self-confidence, one would have to say that the role played by the abstract concept in narration and in description differs more in degree than kind. Nevertheless, precisely the kind of symbolic description Lukács complains of is central in Faulkner's apprentice novels. Meaning in these works is largely conveyed by a play of verbal images that goes on independently of the situation of the characters. It is not that the objects represented in the world and described in often elaborate and highly poetic language cease to have any function in the characters' lives. Rather, that function is plainly subordinate to the place of the object within the symbolic design of the text as a whole. Actions, objects, persons, and verbal images become fundamentally equivalent and interchangeable components, existing on a single plane and constituted with meaning by their relation to the writer's visionary concept. Foreground and background merge, for both take on meaning from their relation to a transcendental plane that is equally distant from either.

That Faulkner's early fiction belongs to Lukács's descriptive mode is not the result of a purely technical decision or a failure of skill. Faulkner fully intends his early novels to be like his poems in deriving their meaning primarily from a relation to a visionary absolute rather than from ordinary human situations. Joseph Blotner tells us that Balzac was one of the writers the young Faulkner most admired (*Faulkner: A Biography*). But Faulkner's sensibility was not initially so attuned to presenting the rough-hewn "truth about people" for which he later praised Balzac; instead his early fiction betrays more attention to "truth in a chalice," the concern for elegantly symbolic language and for the artful contrivance of images, surfaces, and details that he identifies in part with Flaubert. Hence Faulkner tends to fashion his early fictional texts as single complex symbolic landscapes. Dialogue, plot, character, and milieu all become elements in a large, painterly still life. . . .

For all the advances it represents over the early fiction, *The Sound and the Fury* adheres to many of the goals and assumptions articulated in *Mosquitoes*, and there is reason to believe that the book began as an attempt to practice them unequivocally. Faulkner's numerous comments about the composition of *The Sound and the Fury* consistently emphasize the things in it that most resemble his earlier, image-based art. (To many of his readers and critics, Faulkner's convictions about the intentions and achievements of the novel have seemed curiously at odds with the actual text, but for the moment we are interested only in how the book can be seen to resemble his earlier work.) In virtually every statement Faulkner made in thirty years of speaking about the gestation of the novel, he insisted that it began with the luminous image of Caddy Compson and with the situation on the day of Damuddy's death. As Caddy was envisioned in the pastoral landscape at the branch and later peering in at the funeral, she became for Faulkner an image of the ideal beauty so often envisioned in the poetry. "To me she was the beautiful one, she was my heart's darling. That's what I wrote the book about . . . to try to tell, try to draw the picture of Caddy."

Notice that Faulkner abandons a narrative term, "tell," for a pictorial one. The goal remains the drawing of the static image. To the extent that his aim in *The Sound and the Fury* is primarily "to make myself a beautiful and tragic little girl," the book operates under the older method. It seeks an ideal beauty through a single fixed and splendid image, Caddy Compson as a little girl on a particular day. As in the poetry, this ideal is to be seen only indirectly. We see her only through the eyes of her brothers. More important, we discover her significance not directly through the effects on them of her presence but indirectly and negatively through the suffering and intense longing occasioned by her absence.

Moreover, the conception of the scenes on the day of Damuddy's death suggests the pictorial method of *Soldiers' Pay*. At the branch and later outside the Compson house, the children are arranged in a tableau of postures and spatial relationships with Caddy at the center. Very little occurs in the novel to modify the tableau; we get the essential, unchanging meaning of each character in a scene occurring twenty years before most of the others in the novel. Jason's moral isolation and his self-defeating selfishness are visible in his posture, hands jammed in his pockets, and later when he trips over his own feet. Quentin's futile desire to protect and to dominate his sister appears in his reaction to her wetting her dress and in his constant lagging behind in resistance to her leadership. Benjy's dependence on Caddy is evident when she squats in the water before him to soothe and hush his fears. Lastly, Caddy's tenderness is represented by the affectionate attention to Benjy, and her boldness by the insistence on climbing the tree to view the funeral.

The tableau is partly duplicated on a completely different level by the structural relationships of the novel's first three sections. Carried to completion, the duplication would contribute to a singularly static and self-enclosed method. Even as we moved through the three sections, we would proceed as though from one vantage point to another on a grouped configuration of statues, only to find that our steps have traced that very configuration. From each of the vantage points, so Faulkner insists, the intent is to give us an increasingly clearer view of Caddy and the ideal she represents.

In fact, Caddy becomes less important in each successive part of the novel. But her decreasing centrality does not necessarily compromise the centrality of the ideal. Even in Benjy's section, Caddy's significance is manifested most forcefully in the intense pain he feels at her absence. The other three sections are equally devoted to showing the pain caused by loss and absence, including but not limited to the absence of Caddy. The closely parallel emotional patterns in the novel's four sections are emphasized in a striking essay by Carey Wall ("*The Sound and the Fury:* The Emotional Center"). Wall insists on the importance of states of feeling and sequences of emotion even at the expense of their causes and the concrete circumstances surrounding them. Her essay is implicitly directed against more orthodox readings of the novel, which find in it situations, issues, and events that need to be explained. A novel which truly adhered to the old method and focused on creating emotional intensities would, like a Swinburne poem, be singularly resistant to such an explication of content. Details and circumstances would not matter much; the particularities of each brother's situation and the objective conditions of the world the Compsons live in would fade before the common intensity of their suffering and the absent radiance at the center of each monologue. Quentin's anguished debate with his father over the meaning of life would be only an extended sign for the same thing expressed by the battered slipper and the smells of honeysuckle, gasoline, and camphor.

We would thus have a visionary novel based on images of absence, tableaulike configurations, and patterns of emotion, all signifying a pure, fleeting essence of beauty and wholeness.

This is not what most readers and critics have found in *The Sound and the Fury*, a book that after all seems to have something intelligible to say about the world. Yet the novel's obvious themes—the decay of the Old South, the human response to time and change, the relation of childhood experience to adult behavior—are no more exclusively the business of the book than the evocation of a visionary ideal is. Such themes are among the ones expressed by the new method, which seems virtually to be born within the pages of the novel. But although *The Sound and the Fury* inaugurates the new method, it does not embrace it fully or even with the tenacity of the stories and novels that follow shortly afterward.

The seeds of the new method can be noticed in the closing pages of *Mosquitoes*. Fairchild's final pronouncement on the question of art introduces a newly temporal aspect to the speculations. He celebrates the still-to-be-desired "instant of timeless beatitude" but places it in mute, unexplained, apposition to "the Passion Week of the heart." With the advantage of hindsight we can observe here the first small step toward a new idea of the artistically meaningful. It is made possible by Fairchild's connecting two kinds of time, the momentary instant of timeless beatitude in which visionary ideals may be glimpsed and the historical duration of a Passion Week, whose significance derives also from the dramatic conflict occurring within it. The almost casual linking Fairchild makes is a slender enough clue, but it offers the first possibility of understanding temporal existence to be as meaningful as eternal essence. The link is made firm by Faulkner's new use of arrested motion. Occasionally in *Sartoris / Flags in the Dust*, and more assiduously in *The Sound and the Fury*, Faulkner focuses on the process of seeking the visionary realm. As he does, arrested motion comes to represent more than the fundamental artistic vision and the goal of all true works of art. Faulkner begins to attend to the activity, the process of arresting motion, as well as the result. Arresting motion emerges as an object of representation potentially as significant for art as arrested motion, the otherworldly essence sought by the poet or the faun.

Like the yearning for beauty and splendor in "New Orleans," this activity occurs in the everyday world. Indeed, a character's wanting to arrest motion henceforth becomes the principal metaphor for all such yearnings. Therefore when Horace Benbow or one of the Compson brothers tries to halt the motion of life, the attempt is both meaningful in itself and an instance of a universally significant activity. Arresting motion becomes an immanently meaningful action. In *Soldiers' Pay* Faulkner had had something to describe, "the longing of mankind for a Oneness with Something, somewhere," and he portrayed it in a static, pictorial composition. Beginning primarily in *The Sound and the Fury,* he has something to narrate, the attempts of the characters to arrest motion, envisioned as a dynamic interaction between an arresting consciousness and a fluid, phenomenal environment.

The fundamental step here is toward objectifying and externalizing the subjective practices of the poetry. Faulkner's poetic quest for timeless beauty and significance becomes the characteristic action of the people in his fiction. At first the action is meaningful only in terms of the goal that will make it unnecessary; the quest for eternal essence is significant because the ideal is not immediately present in the world. Increasingly, however, arresting motion is meaningful on its own. This opens the way for a reversal of the poetry's manner of generating meaning. The pure quest for the ideal is modulated by attention to the quest as an event with important implications in and for the temporal world. The visionary ideal begins to be displaced by the envisioning of it and the symbol by the symbolizing. The four successive parts of *The Sound and the Fury* can, in fact, be read as stages in just such a displacement. The crucial issue is the status of the ideal. Once the search for it becomes significant in itself and the world of time is granted its own priority, Faulkner's art need no longer depend so utterly on a vision of transcendence. Thus what begins by validating the temporal world as a kind of staging area from which the ideal is sought may end by testing the desire for the ideal against its effects on temporal existence.

Few such doubts about the necessity of an ideal realm are manifest in Benjy's section, which in isolation is the one most governed by the older method. The single image and the timeless ideal are still the centers for the section in which, Faulkner assures us, "the story is all there." Faulkner recognizes fully that Benjy is "like something eyeless and voiceless which might have lived, existed merely because of its ability to suffer." This is exactly why he is so useful as a center of consciousness; his suffering is an unequivocal index of the absence of the ideal. At least to begin with, Benjy is not the moral touchstone that some critics have seen him as; his demands upon the world are as absolute and impossible as those of his brothers. Instead, Benjy is a touchstone for identifying an ideal world and a means of demonstrating its overriding importance. For Benjy the image of Caddy, that of a world of beauty and plenitude, is a purely external thing which is either given or withheld. Because he has never matured from the time at which she meant so much to him, both the full radiance of her presence and the intense agony of her absence continue to be maintained as the simple timeless conditions of a wholly objective world.

In other words, because Benjy is so much the passive register of events, very little intervenes to divert us from the atemporal image of Caddy around which his world organizes itself. To a far greater degree than in the later sections, the stream of consciousness in Benjy's section is instrumental, a means for the expression of the ideal, rather than an intrinsically significant activity of the mind. The focus is not displaced toward the perceiving and imagining and shaping activities that dominate Quentin's and Jason's inner lives. The significance of the nonchronological storytelling in this part does not lie solely in the wish to represent the mental life of an idiot plausibly. It lies also in the principled refusal to temporalize the expression of what is fundamentally and radically atemporal, the vision that Caddy represents to Benjy.

Benjy's status as a passive register is by no means unqualified, however. The seeds of a displacement already exist in his narrative, and they are brought into sharper relief by the way later sections encourage us to reinterpret the first one. Benjy is fully capable of recognizing absence, though not the change which brought it about, and to a limited extent he works to alleviate the pain of absence. Just as he moves in the company of his nurses to the gate, the swing, and the pasture—scenes of remembered presence—so his mind continually returns to the day of his renaming and the day of Damuddy's death. If the movement of his consciousness is no willed escape into a more comforting past, because Benjy hardly distinguishes between past and present and only barely possesses a conscious will, it is at least an instinctive leaning toward pleasant sensations.

In Quentin's section the significance of the narrator's attempt to shape his world is more pronounced. The one-dimensional contrast between presence and absence in Benjy's section is replaced by a more complex conflict between the actualities of the world and the ideals Quentin demands of it. The ideal is not represented for Quentin in given, objective images; rather it is something he is struggling to find or create or reestablish images of. Thus his quest serves as a way of expressing a complaint about the world he lives in. Quentin insists on the radical distinction between eternal essence and temporal existence which is assumed in the poetry. Like the speakers of many of the poems, he demands that things have significance exclusively in terms of the eternal. As Quentin, his father, and almost all critics of the novel agree, Quentin's enemy is time. Because he is so deeply aware of this, his narrative demands a privileged position in the novel. He articulates the frustration about time and change and decay which his brothers can only experience.

Nothing can be meaningful for him if it is not permanent and absolute. "If people could only change one another forever that way merge like a flame swirling up for an instant then blown cleanly out along the cool eternal dark." But Quentin recognizes all too well that everything he sees and does is impermanent, ambiguous, and temporal. He understands to his sorrow that ideals find no objective confirmation in the world; they are only ideals. The material world therefore becomes a storehouse of images which mock his desire for the ideal. Every reflection of the world—including his own shadow, all black persons, and even the memories of his own attempts to implement his ideals—conspires to mock him. In the poems, twilight is often the time when the visionary realm is most discernable, and to Quentin also it offers a "quality of light as if time really had stopped for a while." But twilight is actually the worst time of all for him, because it commingles the ideal and the actual so grotesquely, demanding recognition of their incompatibility. "Down a long corridor of grey halflight where all stable things had become shadowy paradoxical all I had done shadows all I had felt suffered taking visible form antic and perverse mocking without relevance inherent themselves with the denial of the significance they should have affirmed."

Quentin's complaint about the world is itself an indication of displacement. By shifting attention away from the timeless ideal, the novel moves toward taking the temporal world seriously as artistic material. More importantly, the dramatization of the quest serves to particularize and temporalize the ideal realm, to present it as a phenomenon of the imperfect world of everyday life. However much Quentin's ideals are pure and universal, we are shown that they also proceed directly from his personal, worldly idiosyncracies. This serves to diminish the claim made by Quentin (and by Faulkner in the poetry) about their significance. Quentin wants to see himself as a knight of the ideal, challenging or spurning the temporal world in the name of pure ideals. But the particularity of his situation compromises the purity of the quest. His ideals spring from an intensely personal situation, as does his failure to attain them. Although virginity is a traditional enough symbol of uncorrupted essence, the excessive importance Quentin attaches to it is clearly also the result of his neurotic dread of sexuality. "It seemed to me that I could hear whispers secret surges smell the beating of hot blood under wild unsecret flesh watching against red eyelids the swine untethered in pairs rushing coupled into the sea." Likewise, the loss of Caddy is not simply a sign of lost beauty and wholeness, as it is for Benjy. It is also an image of Quentin's personal inability to control his world, either physically by making his sister obey or metaphysically by dictating what the significance of her behavior will be. She is as much the opponent in his struggle to demand timeless significance as she is the object of the struggle. He is still trying to say to her and to the world, "Im stronger than you."

Quentin wants to believe himself a "man of courage" who is faithful enough to his ideals to be willing to die for them. His watery grave will then be the longed-for world of purity, another version of the exclusive hell with its "*clean flame the two of us more than dead.*" As is true of death in many of the poems, the death Quentin imagines for himself will be the attainment of a region where things truly "finished themselves." Even Christ on Judgment Day will be unable to command him to rise, so utter and absolute will be his drowning. Yet for all these heroic posturings, Quentin is obsessed by and unable to refute his father's contention that the only thing that could drive his son to suicide would be a recognition of weakness and failure. "No you will not do that until you come to believe that even she was not quite worth despair." Only out of a fear that he is not strong enough to maintain his private symbols of the ideal permanently will he resort to suicide—so, just before he leaves to do the deed, Quentin hears his father predicting.

The question in all this is how we are to take Quentin's vision of the ideal and his failure either to attain it or to find some way of living without it. Quentin's plight is in some ways universal but in all ways personal. On the one hand, his complaint about the world is surely offered as something to be taken quite seriously, and its accuracy is confirmed by the rest of the novel. This is precisely what Mark Spilka recognizes in an essay in which he struggles manfully to rescue Quentin's narrative from the genre of case history ("Quentin Compson's Universal Grief"). But at the same time Quentin's failure to attain the ideal and even his need to do so are depicted as uniquely and neurotically his own. The effect is to temporalize the ideal, to blur the radical distinction between the eternal and the temporal by showing that the desire for timeless essence is governed by particularity and temporality.

We are thus not quite allowed to see Quentin as a representative protagonist in the human quest for beauty and significance. This is of course how the speakers of the poems ask to be seen, but the objectification and ironic distancing accomplished in Quentin's section supplies an implicit critique of these poems as deluded and sentimental. What does seem representative about Quentin's plight is the genuine intensity of the pain he suffers. His intellect and his sensitivity thus function as equivalent to Benjy's idiocy; they establish a further register of the pain of loss and absence.

By the time we reach Jason's section the displacement may appear almost complete. The concentration on the narrator's activity, his attempt to control his world by word and deed, seems undiluted by a vision of an ideal realm where such arduous struggles are unnecessary. Jason does not even seem to share the kind of anguish which dominates his brothers' monologues; certainly the loss of Caddy does not loom for him as it does for them. He believes that he has been shrewd enough to cut his losses and even to be receiving compensation for them. His financial chicanery, particularly the embezzlement of his niece's money, and the pleasures of cruelty to such as Caddy and Luster are nearly equitable recompense for the purely secular losses he will admit to. The acceptance of such compensation, so Jason (and Faulkner by ironically pronouncing him sane in the "Compson Appendix") argues, is evidence of his superiority to the self-defeating Compson sentimentality.

Much of the horror and also the satiric force of the portrayal of Jason derives from the pettiness of his confessed emblem of loss, the job at Herbert Head's bank, in comparison to his brothers' symbols. No pure ideal seems to attach to Jason's desires or to be signified by his evident pain and frustration. Yet the deeper horror of Jason's situation is the extent to which loss of the job substitutes for a more intense and emotional loss. It is not simply that Jason's desires make his brothers' look noble in contrast; it is that his desires have been twisted so as to deny the emotional needs all three have in common. For Jason also indicates, despite himself, that an earlier, repressed source of his pain is the absence of love and stability in the family. As with Benjy and Quentin, the positive ideal is located in childhood, but for Jason it is not Caddy who is the center but his father and namesake.

Twice Mrs. Compson reproaches Jason for speaking bitterly of his father. Yet Jason's scorn, like Quentin's horror over Caddy's loss of honor, is rooted in a feeling that an ideal has failed him. The almost hysterical concern for his own current position as a quasi-father in the household and the half-admitted sorrow he expresses at Mr. Compson's funeral suggest that behind this scorn is a disappointed image of the father as an anchor of meaningfulness in a healthy family. Most of Jason's numerous references to his father reflect the bitterness; all of them presuppose the importance to him of the ideal father who is not alcoholic, who does not let the fortune and status of his family decline, and who does not love Caddy and Quentin more than Jason.

Jason's sorrow for the loss of this ideal father, the father he wanted or expected or once believed Mr. Compson to be, is obliquely revealed at Mr. Compson's funeral. "We stood there, looking at the grave, and then I got to thinking about when we were little and one thing and another and I got to feeling funny again, kind of mad or something." Jason is embarrassed and uncomfortable about the sentiment, admitting it only by saying several times that he feels "funny." He overcomes the emotion only by performing an otherwise gratuitous act of cruelty, swindling Caddy about seeing her child. The horror of this act, at first glance about the nearest thing to motiveless malignity we see in Jason, reveals both the intensity of his feeling and the way he typically deals with such emotions: transferring them to the loss of the bank job, punishing someone for this loss, and seeking financial compensation for it. "And so I counted the money again that night and put it away, and I didn't feel so bad. I says I reckon that'll show you. I reckon you'll know now that you cant beat me out of a job and get away with it." He congratulates himself that he has advanced beyond the trusting sentimentality of his youth. "I was a kid then. I believed folks when they said they'd do things. I've learned better since."

Jason's narrative is a record of his attempt to control a world he can no longer trust. His unflagging and almost completely unsuccessful struggle is to establish by stength of will a fixed order of behavior in the household. Once the fixity is assured he will at last be able to rest in "peace and quiet" in the place of the esteemed father. Hence his anxiety over the town's opinion of his family and his frantic (and from the reader's perspective, deeply ironic) insistence to his mother about observing the forms of family decorum: "As long as I am buying food for people younger than I am, they'll have to come to the table to eat it. . . . I cant have all this whoop-de-do and sulking at mealtimes. I know that's a lot to ask her, but I'm that way in my own house. Your house, I meant to say."

Jason's self-presentation unwittingly accomplishes a satiric exposure of his belief that he can and does control his world by force of will and by a pragmatic readiness to accept compensation for his daily reverses. Jason's beliefs are as self-defeating as their opposite, the passivity and absolutism that both Benjy and Quentin display. In the "Appendix," it is almost as if Faulkner had taken pity on Jason and granted him his paltry success. He is allowed to live a "domestic, uxorious, connubial" weekend life with his Memphis whore, a situation in which familial stability is assured by the good money Jason pays for it.

The first three sections of *The Sound and the Fury* form an obvious unit unto themselves, each a transcription of the mind of one of the Compson brothers living in the temporal world and seeking in some way to attain a timeless one. The prestige of the timeless ideal declines continuously throughout the first three sections, until little remains in Jason's of the pure, noble plenitude experienced by Benjy and demanded by Quentin. For each brother the ideal is a projection from childhood; for each it derives from a need, increasingly portrayed as sentimental, neurotic, or self-deceiving, to reconstitute an image of the past. But even after the displacement of the desired ideal from Benjy's objective and radiant world of presence, the distinction between the two realms, the timeless and the temporal, continues to be posited. The timeless is increasingly implicated in the temporal as an extension or projection of personal needs, but to the consciousness of each brother, it remains distinct, a world which is other than and elsewhere from what exists.

The final section of the novel, written in the third person, marks the final displacement of the ideal and the most undiluted commitment of the novel to the world of existence. Consciousness as such recedes from view, and we witness for the first time the materiality of the world. The shift is heralded in the opening image of the section, where the weather is shown "precipitating" a "substance" like "minute and venomous particles" on Dilsey's flesh. The passage depicts the impingement of hostile forces on the self, and this, of course, is essentially what all three previous sections had portrayed. Now, however, the radical distinction between the interiority of the self and the exteriority of the world disappears. To Quentin the emanations of the self—shadows, reflections, and memories—had threatened to become part of the alien substance of the temporal world which mocked the ideals so carefully guarded in the mind. Now self and world are not alien to each other; both are seen principally as substance behaving in time.

Substance is portrayed as lasting and yet bearing prominently the marks of time, like the "patina, as though from the soles of bare feet in generations," of the earth around Dilsey's cabin door. Dilsey herself is so much fleshy substance scarred by time and yet enduring within it, "as though muscle and tissue had been courage or fortitude which the days or the years had consumed until only the indomitable skeleton was left rising like a ruin or a landmark above the somnolent and impervious guts." Later we see the tears slide down her pitted cheeks "in and out of the myriad corruscations of immolation and abnegation and time." Her eroded substance participates in the action which is the last section's exclusive focus, the struggle to cope with the temporal weathering to which all is subject. For the marks of time on her flesh are not simply scars representing time's inevitable victories, but corruscations, points of incandescence that represent resistance to the erosion.

The action narrated in the first three sections is primarily mental, the action of consciousness in the world. But consciousness in the last section is no longer something apart. It is no longer private and remote, no longer capable of hoarding a precious image of the ideal and devoted to this task. The narrator reports the contents of Jason's mind no differently than the contents of niece Quentin's bedroom. All is part of temporal existence, and all signifies something important about the concrete situation of human life in a particular time and place. Temporal existence emerges as fully meaningful in itself and not merely a means of passage or a mocking contrast to the pure ideals of consciousness.

The timeless ideal is incorporated into the last section in the promise of Christian salvation implicit in Reverend Shegog's sermon. One may without too great violence to the text read the last section as an endorsement of Christian ideals. Such a reading would assimilate the novel to the celebration of less peculiarly religious ideals which Faulkner's poems and his earlier novels accomplish by somewhat different means. According to such a reading, the Passion Week of the heart would derive its meaning wholly from the transcendent realm for which it is a worldly preparation. Correspondingly, one would find in Faulkner's art another of the many aesthetic programs based on a theory of incarnation, the Logos of Christ serving as the exemplary bridge between time and eternity.

Yet for an Easter sermon Reverend Shegog's is curiously lacking in emphasis on the Resurrection. He dwells instead on suffering in the temporal world and on the generations passing away. The refrain of his sermon is "I got the recollection and the blood of the Lamb." In other words, I maintain in the awareness of my own suffering and in my own ravaged bodily substance a share in the pains of Jesus's life on earth. Dilsey and the rest of the congregation are asked to share the memory of the worldly pains of Jesus and Mary and to do so almost without reference to the eternal realm promised to those who remember and believe. Rather than depending primarily on a transcendental, theological sanction for its obviously beneficial effects, the service celebrates a worldly existence that gains its deepest significance and becomes most bearable when it is recognized as part of a collective suffering with a long and honorable past. Such recognition is what the episode explicitly dramatizes when the individual members of the congregation join together in the service and when they come to include in their midst the memory of all the previous generations.

This is not to say that the specific religious context of the sermon has no importance, only that the issue is not Christianity as such nor even a less doctrinal vision of an eternal realm. It is often asserted that Dilsey, unlike the Compson brothers, sees the present as part of a continuum that includes both time and eternity. "I seed de beginnin, en now I sees de endin." This seems true enough, although the ending she sees here is apparently the end of the Compson household and not a vision of glory. But the specific nature of her beliefs is not that essential; certainly Faulkner supplies only the most sketchy details. What is important is that the beliefs are measured by her behavior in the temporal world. True or false, inspired or illusory, the ideals celebrated in the service provide an "annealment" of Dilsey's ravaged substance. Her indomitable skeleton is enabled to go on resisting consumption. What signifies about Dilsey is the way she behaves in trying to preserve the family, her actions in resistance to the consuming power of time. Belief in Christianity is one of her means of accepting and dealing with the world, and the belief is applauded precisely to the extent it enables her to do so.

To weigh the ideal for its effect on the temporal directly reverses Faulkner's initial method, which was to represent the temporal as a means of demonstrating the necessity of the ideal. Dilsey, who emerges as a substitute for Caddy at the center of the household and a displacement of her, is a concrete representation of the meaningfulness of temporal existence rather than a poetic symbol of the absolute. Dilsey's actions are meaningful as a way of living in time, not as a strategy for escaping it. To conceive Dilsey's life as fit material for art is to forgo the visionary quest for splendid and timeless beauty, or rather to redefine utterly what is meant by such beauty. The Passion Week of the heart, a struggling in time to cope with time, reveals itself as suitable material for the artist. Faulkner's method then becomes very much the traditional art of the novel, a narration of day-to-day existence in which are to be found immanently significant human conflicts.

The method of the last section is not, of course, the method of *The Sound and the Fury* as a whole. The intensity of the yearning for the ideal in the earlier sections is hardly abolished by Dilsey's resolute struggle with the here and the now or by Faulkner's belated discovery of the intrinsic meaningfulness of the human experience of time. We would certainly be perverse in reading Benjy's section as an exposure of a lamentably false consciousness. Dilsey's Christianity does nothing to refute Quentin's vision of a Christ "that not for me died not." "The grave hopeless sound of all voiceless misery under the sun" is still voiced by Benjy at the end, and it can be soothed only by the mechanical arrangement of "each in its ordered place."

Nevertheless, although the yearning for transcendence remains a powerful motive *in* the novel, one too poignantly rendered to be simply a pretext for ironic deflation, it is gradually abandoned as the motive *of* the novel. Objects and characters and events cease to be described (as they so often are in the earlier fiction) as symbols of an otherworldly realm or of the longing to attain it. Instead they are presented according to a version of the narrative method made traditional in the nineteenth century as elements whose function in the text and whose significance in the fictional world are determined by the human experience of time. The static image sought for in the composition of the earlier work gets replaced by a representation of process and motion. The result in *The Sound and the Fury* is a work poised between the visionary and the realistic. But the very juxtaposition of the two is on the side of the new method as Faulkner now conceives it, for it is a means of objectifying and dramatizing the conflict between them.

*T*he Sound and the Fury: A Logic of Tragedy

Warwick Wadlington

In the same year that Joseph Wood Krutch made his famous claim that tragedy was contrary to the modern temper, William Faulkner published a paradoxical refutation. Krutch sought to define and decry his age by appealing to a traditional standard. *The Sound and the Fury* shows that the standard of tragedy contains the logic of its own failure. Yet critics have typically discussed the novel as if it could be described by some comparatively stable model, apart from the debate over the possibility of tragedy.

In the post-Enlightenment, pathos has become the term of contradistinction to tragedy. According to the most widespread view, tragedy involves suffering that results mainly from the protagonist's action, which is usually persistent, decisive—heroic. The mode of pathos, by contrast, is said to involve a relatively passive suffering, not springing from action but inflicted by circumstances. In terms of the linked root meanings of pathos (passion, suffering), tragedy is held to be pathos resulting from heroic action.

The stress on action, legitimized by Aristotle's poetics and ethics, was part of the general cultural defense of responsible human endeavor from the philosophy of mechanistic determinism. For many, the horror of a universe of mere physical motion could be summed up as an oppressive passivity in which, as Matthew Arnold wrote, "there is everything to be endured, nothing to be done." The emphasis on the difference between

From *American Literature* 53, no. 3 (November 1981). © 1981 by Duke University Press.

tragedy and pathos—that is, between action and passivity—was thus fundamentally polemic in nature if not always in tone. By the beginning of Faulkner's career, tragedy had become *the* prestigious literary genre. Pathos had largely lost its neutral, descriptive connotation and was increasingly a term of denigration, especially in the form "pathetic." Influential theorists like the New Humanists upheld a conservative position by accentuating this difference. "Tragic" had become a weapon useful for excoriating the naturalists, the "Freudians," and "the school of cruelty." Yet important writers since at least Dostoevsky had reflected the modern idea of passive man while also seeking to reformulate the possibilities of human action. Sometimes these possibilities were found at the very center of apparent passivity, where pathos is describable by its etymological kin, pathology.

But action is not the only usual discriminator of tragedy. In Aristotle's account, the mimesis of action arouses in the audience certain passions and subjects them to catharsis. A catastrophe is instrumental in effecting this tragic relief. In pathos, by contrast there is no final crisis, no resolution and emotional disburdening. Passion is the inconclusive fate.

The traditional conception (or kind) of tragedy we consider here focuses typically on the drastic either/or to which life may be reduced, in a tightening spiral of narrowing options. *Antigone, Hamlet, Moby-Dick,* and *The Mayor of Casterbridge*, for example, follow this pattern, as does the *Oresteia* until the last-moment reversal. Hegel's theory speaks powerfully to such cases by treating tragedy as the collision of contradictory views. In Hegel's Absolute, variances are merely *differences,* but when concretized in human action they become contradictory *oppositions* liable to tragic conflict.

Hegel aside for the moment, the idea of contradictory opposition itself points to connections between pairs of concepts that seem simply opposed— the modern temper and the heroic, and tragedy and pathos. In *The Heroic Temper,* Bernard Knox authoritatively defines the hallmark of Sophocles' tragic heroes: "Their watchword is: 'he who is not with me is against me.' " Sophoclean tragedy dramatizes the usually unavailing attempts of advisors to persuade the intransigent heroes—Ajax, Antigone, Electra, Oedipus, Philoctetes—to abandon the self-destructive polarization of their outraged self-esteem against the world. The Sophoclean heroic outlook is the relatively rare consequence of a severe threat to personal worth that arouses the exceptional person to this uncompromisingly dichotomous attitude. Let us imagine a case, however, in which the essential binary quality of this temper became widespread. Such would be the result if dichotomy were the usual structure of consciousness. The protagonist then would be surrounded by those who, at bottom, experience life in no less starkly divisive terms than he or she does on the tragic occasion. Rather than being a monitory, awe-inspiring anomaly as in Sophocles, polarization would be a constant daily potential. The result would be strikingly different from Sophoclean tragedy, though bearing the prototype's mark. The ironic product is the odd suspension of heroic temper and "unheroism" in tone and mood of *The Sound and the Fury*.

In a traditional conception like Hegel's, tragedy advances through the revelation of oppositions to their resolution. Faulkner's novel, however, probes to an inchoate, divisive logic of tragedy operating throughout thought and experience. *The Sound and the Fury* relocates the schism of tragedy in a basically dichotomous worldview. And in so doing, it discloses the potential of tragedy to become continuous with its antitype, pathos. Insofar as tragedy conventionally entails resolution, the very ubiquity of tragic schism ironically produces the repetitious, inconclusive situation of tragedy's opposite. Instead of catastrophe, there is repeated disaster.

The Compsons' schismatic, incipiently tragic mental habits are strikingly—though perversely—like a two-value logic. This ordinary formal logic depends upon the Aristotelian law of identity according to which an entity can only be what it is: A is A. Given the assumption of uniform entities, to say that a thing is simultaneously something else violates the law of noncontradiction. This is the logic of arithmetic (which Mr. Compson's language of "sum" and "problem" reflects) in which an answer is always either right or wrong. A characteristic form is the mathematical proof that depends on showing contradiction—the *reductio ad absurdum*. As formal logic, this binary ordering is unexceptionable. As the foundation for a wholesale system of dichotomy taken as the sole orientation to reality, such a logic becomes disastrous. Matters that call for the recognition of compound entities, gradations, and probabilities are continually reduced to the Yes or No of tragic dilemma.

When polarized options are habitual, crisis becomes attrition, and passion a banal repetition. Christ was not crucified, Mr. Compson tells Quentin, but worn away by the minute clicking of time's little wheels. "If things just finished themselves," Quentin thinks at one point. "Again," he concludes, is the "Saddest [word] of all." He yearns for the decisive calamity, some unburdening conclusiveness, however terrible. He yearns, that is, for a kind of tragedy that is not his. Not surprisingly, Quentin has been the primary focus for discussing the novel's tragic dimensions. He will provide our focus as well.

The absence of tragic closure in the novel, then, does not stem from a view that there can be no momentous catastrophe in a modern "everyday" world for reasons unrelated to the tragic process. Such an extrinsic view underlies the opinions of those like Krutch and George Steiner who have analyzed the death of tragedy. Rather, in Faulkner, the binary logic that produces in the first instance the tragic heroic crisis must also eventuate in devastating *everydayness:* tomorrow and tomorrow. . . . Faulkner's title echoes the most famous protest against a life without climax. But Macbeth, by finding his resolving action, diverts his drama from the idiotic tomorrows signifying nothing. The period of Faulkner's great modern tragedies begins with a statement of the disqualification of such tragedy by its own logic. Put concisely, in the words of Quentin's false comforter: "tragedy is second-hand."

II

Quentin's first memory upon waking is of his father giving him Grandfather's watch with the observation that it is "the mausoleum of all hope and desire; it's rather excrutiating-ly apt that you will use it to gain the reducto absurdum of all human experience which can fit your individual needs no better than it fitted his or his father's. I give it to you not that you may remember time, but that you might forget it now and then for a moment and not spend all your breath trying to conquer it." Time and time-consciousness contadict human experience, as the reference to *reductio ad absurdum* indicates. It is, in Mr. Compson's phrase, excruciatingly apt that Quentin's interior monologue begin with this appeal to contradiction, which obsesses Quentin as much as time does. In fact, one obsession is implicit in the other. The association is made overt again when he sees watches in a store window displaying "a dozen different hours and each with the same assertive and contadictory assurance that mine had, without any hands at all. Contradicting one another."

What strikes Quentin about the boys quarreling at the bridge is that their voices are "insistent and contradictory and impatient." He has assimilated his father's habit of thinking in terms of conflicts between assertive irreconcilable opposites, as in Mr. Compson's arithmetical definition of man as the "sum of his climatic experiences. . . . Man the sum of what have you. A problem in impure properties carried tediously to an unvarying nil: stalemate of dust and desire." Again two things—dust and desire—contradict one another in conflict, leaving a "nil." Similarly, to prove to Quentin that Caddy's virginity was always an illusion, Mr. Compson reasons by contradiction: "Women are never virgins. Purity is a negative state and therefore contrary to nature."

Quentin and his father tend to experience difference as contradiction, multiplicity as a stalemated war between "impure properties." The whole novel traces the fault lines of this mental set. A universe of antagonisms is formed, all divided and subdivided, as awareness focuses on each, into further bifurcations of "A and not-A."

This universe appears in the blanket social distinction between the "quality" and the nonquality. The first category is further divided by Mrs. Compson's obsession with the status of Compsons versus that of Bascombs, and the latter heading divided into her ne'er-do-well brother Maury and her son Jason, her "salvation" and a true Bascomb. The binary set informs her belief that "there is no halfway ground that a woman is either a lady or not," as well as Jason's identical idea that "Once a bitch always a bitch." It structures Jason's efforts to apply his commercial scheme of credits and debits to all areas of human relationship. It is resplendent in the moment when he believes his life will reach a heroic climax: "He could see the opposed forces of his destiny and his will drawing swiftly together now, toward a junction that would be irrevocable. . . . There would be just one right thing, without alternatives: he must do that." In this binary universe, as in Hegel's idea of tragic collision, all *distinctions* become *divisions*. Subtly or overtly, the daily craving is Jason's lust for clearly opposed forces, the one right thing to do.

To be immersed into Benjy's perspective, which reduces everything to an unqualified opposition (Caddy and not-Caddy), is our proper introduction to the Compson experience of life. As in the novel's first scene, the mental landscape is without middle ground or nuance—there is only this side of the fence or that side of the fence. Yet Faulkner consistently evokes a luxuriant polysemous wealth. Aside from Benjy's lack of normal organic development, his mental processes differ from those of the rest of the family only in degree, not in kind of simplification. In a sense his schematic is larger than life, but it shows what is in the life.

There can be strength in such a view, for it licenses an exhilarating call to arms, literal or figurative, of friends unified against a monolithic enemy. This ethos in general both attracted Faulkner and aroused his intense suspicion. Benjy's daily existence, however, most incisively illustrates that strength must be followed by impotence as the "enemy" increases and meaning becomes fragile.

Life's myriad variety through time is only experienced under a single undiscriminating rubric of the false (inferior, detrimental, unreal) opposing repeatedly that which is alone true and valuable. In other words, if all differences are opposites, then the opposition will grow very numerous. In compensation for this, as time passes the categories are made ever more rigid and uncompromising. Thus more of life's possibilities are excluded only to reappear as an increased repetition of the negative more insistently battering at one's citadel. In proportion as the impending collapse is suspected, a sound and fury arises in protest and defense. This is the moribund stage of the process, the "loud world" on which the novel concentrates. Benjy's bellow and Mrs. Compson's wail echo Quentin's outraged cry as he attacks the shadowy company of Caddy's seducers in the person of Gerald Bland.

Benjy's scream upon being driven to the left rather than to the right of the Confederate soldier statue is the novel's final instance of the fragility of meaning resulting from dichotomy, "each in its ordered place." To offend against any item is to offend against all, the whole category of right. Living on such terms means being haunted by the vulnerability of the self erected upon this system, and consequently being preoccupied with security. This apprehension flares up startlingly in Quentin's fantasy of his father rushing to deal with Benjy's interruption of Caddy's wedding: *"Father had a V-shaped silver cuirass on his running chest."* The one kind of heroic invulnerability, which brought the dashing Compson forebears to their power, is archaic, grotesquely helpless to deal with what follows from it, as son from father. As time discloses, the impotent pathos is an inherent potential of its seeming contrary of vigorous action. It is not just around the Confederate monument, but in it.

The Compsons' isolation, frequently noted, is more than a historically accurate representation of the separatism of caste society, as are all the images of enclosure and boundaries—fences, gates, streams, doors, locked rooms, prisons. The continual bickering, vengefulness, and whining manifest the nervous strain of the besieged. Quentin's desperate fantasy of incest is in its own way a rigorous extension of the inbreeding attitude of a household that feels itself surrounded by relative nonentities.

All this is why the frequent critical comment that Quentin is not heroic is both correct and not to the main point, as are discussions that begin and end with his pathology. But to see the heroic etiology of Quentin's, and his family's, unheroic condition is to begin to see what kind of work one is reading.

Walter J. Slatoff makes an explicit distinction in Faulkner's works between pathology and tragedy (*Quest for Failure: A Study of William Faulkner*). Often, however, there is a more subtle, implicit tendency among Faulkner's commentators to ignore or downplay the pathological element when discussing the tragic, or vice versa. The other tendency is to use both ideas but fail to confront their problematic relationship, so that the generic term becomes a rather flaccid compliment. One of the best critics of the novel, André Bleikasten, writes at length of "Quentin's tragedy of inheritance," yet "tragedy" seems undeservedly honorific because for Bleikasten "there is of course nothing heroic about Quentin," whose "story can be read as an ironic inversion of the familiar journey of the Romantic ego"(*The Most Splendid Faulure: Faulkner's* The Sound and the Fury). Bleikasten's discussion, seasoned with the words "tragic" and "tragedy," considers pathology alone. He attempts to relate Quentin's weakness to the daunting consciousness of a dominating ancestral figure which prevents Mr. Compson and Quentin from fulfilling their generational roles—both become mere impotent sons of the dead Father. Yet this is a needless reading of the historical dimension of *Absalom, Absalom!* back into *The Sound and the Fury*. There are valuable Freudian insights in Bleikasten's analysis, as in the similar approach of John Irwin. However, in *this* novel we are not presented the debilitating awareness of an ancestral father but a structure of consciousness itself inherited all too faithfully from him and his like, with the decay of the family line intrinsic in it.

In his own way, Mr. Compson tries to counter his family's fixation upon victory or defeat: "Because no battle is ever won. . . . They are not even fought. The field only reveals to man his own folly and despair, and victory is an illusion of philosophers and fools." But this view still manifests an embattled life, in the form of a deadlock paralyzing action. Life is a cold war.

The factuality and calculations we associate not with the heroic but the modern age in reality reflect this cold war of the latter days of heroic action. The fatal dichotomies of value are cut from the same cloth as the binary reduction of value to arithmetic. Quentin's later recollections of the "reducto absurdum" statement show clearly that his father's admonition concerns more than the time-consciousness that critics have stressed. Sardonically, Quentin computes his suicide: "The displacement of water is equal to the something of something. Reducto absurdum of all human experience, and two six-pound flat-irons weigh more than one tailor's goose." In this framework, personal experience is simply another item to be counted; it is, indeed, not *personal,* but a public objective fact. Mr. Compson "understands" the deadly effect on personal hope and desire of a consciousness ruled by number and the hateful siege of contraries. But fittingly, his language contradicts him. The personal human experience he sees imperiled is denatured by his own formula, "sum of climatic experiences."

III

The Compson children seek to escape from the passivity of their suffering, a condition ironically produced by the binary worldview traditionally suited to heroic action. The central, insidious cause of their debility is that this same orientation threatens to alienate them from their own experience. The attempt to reclaim the personal dimension of their lives, consequently, is a deeply purposeful act, a nascent counter to passivity. For Quentin, the crucial issue is his passion.

The implications of a two-value system for passion are considerable. The one-or-nothing of dichotomy is reflected in the heroic gambler heritage of staking all "on a single blind turn of a card," as all do in their conflicting ways. Applied to relationships, this orientation can make for the single-minded loyalty Faulkner esteems highly. The tragic defect of this virtue is the narrow emotional exclusiveness that plagues the Compsons.

For Mrs. Compson the one-and-only who commands her devotion is Jason. Quentin is partly influenced by his maternal abandonment, which he feels acutely, to intensify his attachment to Caddy into fixation. To stake one's emotional life on the turn of one card is to become liable to suffering. But the Compson ethos goes farther in associating emotion with pain. For all the Compson children the emotions have been given the unhealthy tinge of an ordeal or affliction, so that for them we are justified in speaking of passions in the double sense of feeling and suffering. The mother's donning black when Caddy is first kissed can stand for the whole joyless association.

Quentin's nearly stupefied "temporary" punctuates his father's well-meaning argument that time will remove all pain. If Quentin cannot have his exclusive One, Caddy, then he desires a permanent grief over the loss, for at least grief preserves feeling. He has had to learn that feeling is suffering, but then to be faced with the loss of suffering too is unthinkable.

As we saw, there is an inherent tendency in a two-value classification to treat varied negative features of life as an undifferentiated set, as if they constituted the same evil repeated through time. To Benjy, a single agony of loss recurs daily in many guises. In Quentin's more complex version, a broken leg in childhood provides him an index-pain recurring as a gasping "ah ah ah." So too from a broader standpoint the father reassures Quentin that the dishonor of sisters recurs in life, that "tragedy is second-hand." Again the father implicitly devalues Quentin's passion by denying that it is distinctive, individual, no matter how many its analogues. Instead of being his, it is threatened with being unredeemably anonymous, not only derivative but lacking even the distinctive archetype of the Passion: "Father was teaching us that all men are just accumulations dolls stuffed with sawdust swept up from the trash heaps where all previous dolls had been thrown away the sawdust flowing from what wound in what side that had not for me died not." For the father, passion is passive: "a love or a sorrow is a bond purchased without design and . . . matures willynilly and is recalled without warning to be replaced by whatever issue the gods happen to be floating at the time." The father's kind of individualism honors the personal quality of experience only in a passionless integrity: "whether or not you consider [an act] courageous is of more importance than the act itself than any act."

Similar in their experience of time, father and son diverge in their view of emotions. Mr. Compson advocates that the rational person disavow his own passion as time's minion, a weakness and "impure property." His alcoholism is his suicidal tribute to—and Faulkner's comment on—this Stoic aim. The philosophy the father offers ends not by diminishing Quentin's pain but by threatening its significance.

Quentin is faced, then, with the "reducto absurdum" of the objective absolutist approach to life and its mirror image, temporal nihilism. From these perspectives, human experience becomes mere fact as its personal quality is erased: *my* hope, *my* desire, *your* love, and *your* loss become meaningless. The schema that began by making a decisive cut between what was on my side and what was not, concludes by enfeebling the very idea of *mine*. Each character is threatened with a radical dispossession. Benjy and Quentin in particular experience even their own body processes, thoughts, and actions as alienated. The Compson world frustrates the individualism it espouses by a binary orientation that in effect denies basic self-esteem. Despite their aversion to anomaly, the Compsons live this fundamental contradiction. Yet they neither subside into numbness nor yield their stubborn hold on personal value. They continue to grasp both individualism and a self-defeating way of founding it. Although tragedy within their world is "second-hand," we as readers can see in such persistence a necessary element of tragedy.

Among the brothers Compson, this tragic persistence in vindicating the personal includes a tendency to cloistered subjectivism, a habit of self-justification, and a reaction against whatever diminishes uniqueness. Here we find also the cause of their possessiveness. Each brother clutches at something exclusively his, to supply from the public world what is lacking in the private. If *my* experience is alienated, I try to reclaim something I believe mine and wrongly taken from me. This is the truth underlying Jason's rationalization that his greed and thievery are excused by "getting back his own." And Benjy and Quentin each deploy the similar fable of "his" Caddy and her symbolic substitutes as objects of passion. To adopt Faulkner's later comment, such efforts reveal the most basic meaning of "aveng[ing] the dispossessed Compsons" (Appendix).

Caddy, too, for all her rebellion against the family, still dramatizes its orientation when she incites Quentin to think himself her possessor, able to dispose of her as he will, in their scenes by the branch. Indeed, her development recapitulates the family's progression along the continuum from active to passive. The young Caddy who demands that brothers and servants obey her during the period of Damuddy's death, who pushes Natalie down the ladder, fights with Quentin, and dreams of being a general, giant, or king, is the same Caddy who later lies passive under the phallic knife Quentin holds to her throat and acts out a surrender to her imagined sexual "opponent": "yes I hate him I would die for him"; "yes Ill do anything you want me to anything yes . . . she lifted her face then I saw she wasn't even looking at me at all I could see [her eyes'] white rim." At the same time, however, she performs what a psychologist would call a passive aggression, for she controls and "owns" Quentin by her sexual display, especially when he realizes at its climax that she imagines herself in someone else's arms.

According to the Compsons' orientation, the chosen One must be uniform, without the "impure property" represented by the young Caddy's muddy drawers. Further, her many anonymous suitors undermine the idea of possessing her exclusively, distinctively. Thus Quentin is both fascinated and nauseated by sexuality, which subverts instead of supporting his dualism. When he imagines anonymous intercourse, vital boundaries dissolve between an impure "imperious" inner realm and a vulnerable outer: "Then know that some man that all those mysterious and imperious concealed. . . . Liquid putrefaction like drowned things floating like pale rubber flabbily filled getting the odour of honeysuckle all mixed up."

Symbolizing Caddy, twilight above all stands for the mixed, liminal, shadowy phenomena that are ill sorted by binary consciousness. Twilight evokes for Quentin a vision that his doing and suffering are taunted by inadmissable paradox:

> I seemed to be lying neither asleep nor awake looking down a long corridor of grey halflight where all stable things had become shadowy paradoxical all I had done shadows all I had felt suffered taking visible form antic and perverse mocking without relevance inherent themselves with the denial of the significance they should have affirmed thinking I was I was not who was not was not who.

The doubtful self is enervated by the dichotomy that is not so much thought as uncomfortably inhabited, as in the long corridor between the polarized realms of the House of Compson. Made intimate guests there, we can experience, if not assent to, Quentin's conviction: better a suicide that promises, however fantastically, to transform all this.

IV

We have distinguished two phases in the novel's tragic process: the decline of action into passivity, and the attempt at reversal. In the first, Quentin's pathos, both pathological and nonpathological, derives from a logic of tragedy that Faulkner has read back into daily life. In the second, Quentin's effort to reclaim the personal by commitment to his passion creates the passion necessary to tragedy. Passion itself becomes purposeful action and transcends the condition of simple passivity.

Yet this necessary condition of traditional tragedy is not a sufficient condition. Not only is catastrophe lacking, but there is no direct recognition of suffering as sometimes, in effect, substitutes for catastrophe (*Prometheus Bound*) or augments it. In the *Philoctetes,* for example, there is an "audience" within the play, Neoptolemus, whose final acknowledgment, rather than exploitation, of the hero's suffering is the crux of the play, releasing our emotions. But Quentin's personal experience has no standing in the public factual world. The impassive eyes staring at him everywhere on his last day represent the objective "ordered certitude" that "sees injustice done," like the "cruel unwinking minds" in his memory of school children who know the correct facts. Quentin's pain cannot be tragic in this view because, as George Eliot says of Dorothea's tragedy in *Middlemarch,* "we do not expect people to be deeply moved by what is not unusual." It is made maddeningly plain to Quentin that his trouble at a sister's maturity and "dishonor" is too familiarly recurrent in life to be considered unusual. The very aberration—the really unusual form and degree—of his response is exacerbated by his desperation to break out of a vicious circle of the usual. The repetition-bound binary outlook that fosters his pathos also prevents others from certifying that his pain is significant.

Catharsis is thus carefully displaced from Quentin to Dilsey. And Dilsey is not so much an agent whose own suffering is witnessed as she is the novel's central sympathizing—yet in a key sense alienated—witness, audience. Reverend Shegog's Easter sermon, with its contagious refrain "I sees," evokes the one Passion that has sufficient public standing to release the congregation's passions, otherwise "banal" and inexpressible. The communally validated Passion, shut off from Quentin in Dilsey's world, combines with his own thoughts of Christ and his Passion to indicate that

Quentin's death is a bid for tragic recognition. Quentin, in short, improvises his own passion, a suicidal "autogethsemane." Its intended public impact is confirmed by his vision of himself and Caddy in hell: *"the two of us amid the pointing and the horror beyond the clean flame. . . . Only you and me then amid the pointing and the horror walled by the clean flame."* If others cannot sympathize, then their impassivity will be stripped away. In this embattled conclusive suffering, a victory could be claimed for the defiant heroic temper as its passion is witnessed with antipathy.

Quentin's suicide, an act both momentous and his exclusively, is meant as an adequate public sign of his personal experience. But his signal is taken by others as yet another repetition of Compson disaster, their "curse." Within the novel's setting, this symbol lacks empathetic reading. That we will supply this crucial lack is Faulkner's own gamble on creating tragedy in defiance of its instability. For we can view the passion displayed within the book in a way that the characters cannot, and yet the difficulty of the internal monologues necessary for this intimacy challenges our ability to witness. If by now readers can surmount this barrier, another has remained: the common two-value assumption of an unbridgeable division between tragedy and pathos.

V

In keeping with the key role that the ideal of tragedy has played in the controversy over modernist writers like Faulkner, George Marion O'Donnell defended him as a "traditional moralist" who, like Quentin, was always *"striving toward* the condition of tragedy. He is the Quentin Compson . . . of modern fiction."

Since O'Donnell's landmark 1939 essay, a dominant tendency in Faulkner criticism, represented by the invaluable work of Cowley, Warren, and Brooks, has emphasized "the conflict between traditionalism and the anti-traditional modern world in which it is immersed." The conflict is real. In arguing for the dialectical continuity between tragedy and pathos in *The Sound and the Fury,* however, in effect I have argued that here—and I believe in Faulkner generally—the continuity between these worlds is as true and important as the change from one to the other and their conflict. Such a view accords with Faulkner's repeated assertion that certain basic human traits, types, and life-patterns continue throughout history, though constantly in new forms. There is, in fact, a continuity *of* conflict for the inheritors of the heroic temper and its fateful logic.

"Jim Crow" and *The Sound and the Fury*

Thadious M. Davis

The complex problem regarding perception of self and others that is intrinsic to Faulkner's art [is] the intellectual and emotional duality of southerners which is most forcefully revealed in the double standards of race. Having its historical origins in slavery, in postbellum society this duality pertains directly to the spread of "Jim Crow" which insured that the two already existing societies, one white and the other black, would be opposed to each other. Faulkner's fiction relies upon differences between values, attitudes, beliefs, or hopes of white and black life. His characters who most avidly uphold racial distinctions cannot acknowledge a common humanity. Jason, for example, voices one of the commonplace assumptions resulting from this view: "When people act like niggers, no matter who they are the only thing to do is to treat them like a nigger." Jason uses "people" as a synonym for whites. A "nigger," according to Jason's logic, is not a person and so cannot behave as "people."

Because of this fragmented condition, Faulkner's white and black characters develop the ability to live mutually exclusive lives, which acknowledge the existence but not the validity of the other. As a result, they are suspended in moral and intellectual contradictions. They learn to live with a false sense of harmony by partially blinding themselves to reality. Although their separate worlds sometimes show signs of consolidation beyond superficial contact, such signs prove misleading. Faulkner's whites especially are rivetted to rituals and manners; their relationships remain fixed

From *Faulkner's "Negro": Art and the Southern Context*. © 1983 by Louisiana State University Press.

and static. Change is frustrated by impotency and fear—outgrowths of an isolation dictated by historical division. In *The Sound and the Fury,* Faulkner presents the Gibsons seemingly within reach of the Compsons, who need new models for saving themselves; however, he maintains implicitly that the Gibsons are inaccessible to the whites. He suggests that the Compsons cannot learn from the example of the Negro because they do not see the example. The partitioning of their society distorts their vision of life and themselves.

The girl Quentin in her relationship with Dilsey is Faulkner's most dramatic rendering of duality in a divided world. Her contradictory feelings toward the black servant prevent her from receiving the maternal comfort she seeks. In Benjy's section, Dilsey defends Quentin against Jason's insinuations: *"Hush your mouth, Jason, Dilsey said. She went and put her arm around Quentin. Sit down, honey, Dilsey said. He ought to be shamed of hisself, throwing what aint your fault up to you."* But Quentin responds by pushing Dilsey away. And in Jason's monologue, Quentin, stung by Jason's taunt ("You damn little slut"), calls out to Dilsey for comfort: " 'Dilsey', she says, 'Dilsey I want my mother.' Dilsey went to her. 'Now, now,' she says, 'He aint gwine so much as lay his hand on you while Ise here'." Yet when Dilsey touches Quentin, she is immediately rebuffed. Quentin knocks her hand down and cries out, " 'You damn old nigger.' "

Simultaneously, the white girl reaches out for Dilsey as a mother substitute and rejects "the nigger" who could never be her mother. Some part of Quentin is cut off from her immediate emotional response to Dilsey by a detached stereotype of "nigger." Her rebuke reflects the stratification of the world she lives in. The girl is at once strongly attracted to Dilsey's kind support and repulsed by the "old nigger." Despite her adolescent rebelliousness and need for love, Quentin is locked into acceptance of a divided world, which encourages and condones keeping Dilsey in a "nigger's place."

Even more than the other Compsons, Quentin, narrator of "June Second 1910," exemplifies the stultifying results of a fractured world, because in the process of learning to live in that world, he suffers an irreparable fragmentation of self. Quentin is an exaggeration of the southern gentleman, whose mind, no longer creative, is locked into sterile types and kinds, codes and manners. His unfailing attention to details of stylized behavior and custom, even when they lack meaning in social interaction, illustrates the extent of his division. His slavery to social conduct blocks off reality, particularly at the end of his monologue when he brushes his teeth and looks for a freshman hat before going to drown himself. His actions point to an evasion of reality by sacrificing clear perception and honest thinking.

Quentin's thoughts about blacks, however, most clearly reveal that his personality, his pattern of thought and behavior are rigidly shaped by an escape mechanism involving the fragmentation of self. Throughout his monologue Quentin returns time and again to "niggers": Deacon, bootblacks, nigger sayings, anonymous niggers, Louis Hatcher, the Gibsons. Even in the simple matter of getting on northern streetcars, he notices immediately whether or not "niggers" are aboard. Despite his dwelling on blacks and his seeming awareness of them, Quentin still observes, "I used to think that a Southerner had to be always conscious of niggers." He believes that he is not, and the irony lies in the discrepancy between what he believes about himself, and his world, and what his thoughts and actions reveal. Quentin's preoccupation with blacks represents his unacknowledged awareness of the other, alternative possibility for life in a divided world— the world which Quentin as southerner transposes to Massachusetts. The Negro populating Quentin's monologue becomes a strategic figure for what is missing in Quentin's white world and a subtle projection of his own internal state.

Because Faulkner sets the narrative present in this monologue during Quentin's year away from home, he does not rely upon the Gibsons as much as in the other sections. Whereas the black family remains crucial to Quentin's memories of the South, a new black character, the Deacon, achieves prominence in his activities and thoughts in Cambridge. Deacon serves functions similar to those of the Gibsons, but, more importantly, he is Quentin's double. Rather than bearing the youth's social and familial history as the Gibsons do, Deacon carries Quentin's psychological history. He forwards the exposition of Quentin's psyche and the tensions within his self-revelations. With the introduction of Deacon, Faulkner begins an exploration of the Negro as a dark presence creating tensions in the minds of his white characters that attains its greatest significance in later works, particularly *Absalom, Absalom!* and *Go Down, Moses*.

It is thematically and structurally appropriate that Quentin seeks out Deacon on the last day of his life. Deacon emerges directly out of Quentin's troubled thoughts about his father (*"Father behind me beyond the rasping darkness"*). The black man appears in military regalia and offers Quentin a "salute, a very superior-officerish kind," both of which link him to General Compson, Quentin's grandfather. Deacon seems to be a projection of Quentin's cultural past. His allusive figure, all that Quentin has left for farewells, is representative of Quentin's lack of immediate connection with any meaningful present world and his nostalgia for a romanticized past.

Despite his disclaimer of involvement in what Deacon is, Quentin is figuratively bound to Deacon, who knowingly observes, " 'You and me's the same folks.' " Deacon is a manifestation of a side of Quentin's sub-conscious mind which both attracts and repels the white youth. The meeting of the two men establishes the darker, unconscious part of Quentin and makes concrete the burden of his personal and cultural past. Deacon's presence assures Quentin of immortality, because Deacon has mastered adaptation as a method of survival. At the same time, Deacon announces Quentin's suicide by symbolically replacing the chimes and shadows as pronouncements of death. Their meeting is an imaginative restatement of Faulkner's union of blacks and whites: "two opposed concepts antipathetic by race, blood, nature and environment, touching for a moment and fused within the illusion of a contradiction" (*Flags in the Dust*). But in this meeting "the illusion of a contradiction" prevails, because Quentin fails to recognize Deacon's place in his life.

Quentin rightly calls Deacon a natural psychologist. Like the black southerner, Deacon understands the white man's need for the Negro to "see after" him. And because the white southerner's world in Faulkner's fiction depends upon a black presence, Quentin especially seeks out reminders of home and familiar things in that strange, antagonistic setting, "the North." Deacon extorts the maximum dividends from this condition; "he could pick out a Southerner with one glance . . . never missed and once he had heard you speak he could name your state." He skillfully plays to the southerners' assumptions about reality. He greets them in "a sort of Uncle Tom's cabin outfit, patches and all," and he uses the corresponding dialect: "Yes, suh. Right dis way, young marster, hyer we is.' " Deacon astutely recognizes a need and so fills it without qualms about prostituting himself. He appears to be the loyal, fawning darky servant at first, and he is—but only for his own ends. The one suspect part of his initial performance is that he loads the luggage onto a fifteen-year-old white youth, who is actually Deacon's pack animal and delivery boy. The white boy should be the southerners' clue that all is not what it appears to be with Deacon, but their training has not been to examine the Negro closely. And so for forty years, each new group continues to be duped upon arrival: "he had you completely subjugated he was always in or out of your room, ubiquitous and garrulous, though his manner gradually moved northward as his raiment improved, until at last when he had bled you until you began to learn better he was calling you Quentin or whatever, and when you saw him next he'd be wearing a cast-off Brooks suit."

Despite his observation of the gradual change in Deacon's manner and appearance, Quentin is not prompted to revaluate himself and his south-ernness in relationship to the ritual drama Deacon instigates. Deacon stands for the stubborn unreality of Quentin's world and his approach to life. For Quentin, Deacon recalls the "reality" of the South for which he is about to commit suicide. Deacon is hollow and substanceless like that reality; he is not only illusive, but also a successful perpetrator of "chicanery" and "hypocrisy" (terms Quentin applies to Deacon). Yet, importantly, Deacon is a man who knows how to cope with life. He chooses life over death, even if life involves compromise.

Just as Gerald Bland and his mother, the wealthy Kentuckians who constantly evoke the Old South in anecdotes of "Gerald's horses and Gerald's niggers and Gerald's women," are conventional types of southern characters, so is Deacon, the trickster, with his multiple costumes and guises. Deacon seems to be an extension of the black fugitive slave in antislavery fiction who, under various disguises, hides his "true identity" in order to escape the South and survive. He prefigures the modern hustler-trickster, such as Ralph Ellison's Rinehart, a northern black of many guises in *Invisible Man* (1952). Deacon's message is adaptation: take what is useful from the old and transform it into the new.

However, Deacon is as incomprehensible to Quentin as the rest of the North and South, at least partly because Quentin's mental training in a divided world has been in terms of blacks being like other blacks and whites being like other whites. He can view Deacon's devices for survival only as objectionably "Negro." Thus Quentin makes an inevitable mistake; he looks at Deacon and sees, not himself, but Roskus: "His eyes were soft and irisless and brown, suddenly I saw Roskus watching me from behind all his whitefolks' claptrap of uniforms and politics and Harvard manner; diffident, secret, inarticulate and sad." Quentin does not recognize the basis for his closeness to Deacon. He lacks the ability to be meaningfully self-critical, because as a southerner drawn to the old order of the South, Quentin suffers from the inability to identify himself with the Negro or to analyze himself in terms of what he finds there. Deacon symbolizes the lost, or missed, opportunity for personal integration in Quentin himself. Quentin fails, therefore, to see his own reflection ("diffident, secret, inarticulate and sad") in Deacon, even though he recognizes in another instant: "Roskus was gone. Once more he was the self he had long since taught himself to wear in the world's eye, pompous, spurious, not quite gross." Quentin has also taught himself to wear in the world's eye a romantic self that is "pompous, spurious," a somewhat Byronic self that is as well "not quite gross."

Quentin and Deacon are linked by their pretenses and self-deceptions. Both men wear masks and play absurd roles; Quentin's is foisted upon him by his southern past; Deacon chooses his, though its archetype is found in the past. Both characters live lies, shape their existences to them, and believe in them in spite of themselves. Quentin desires to go beyond this position and force others to believe the lie too; Deacon is content merely to have others tolerate it. Quentin's failure makes death attractive because death captures the essence of an existence he has felt compelled to make actual in life. Such convoluted reasoning becomes another reflection of Quentin's confusion and his fragmentation.

At the same time, Quentin makes the seemingly penetrating observation "that a nigger is not a person so much as a form of behavior; a sort of obverse reflection of the white people he lives among." That "nigger" is a social creation is insightful, but Quentin's generalization does not suggest that "nigger" is the white man's way of seeing the black man. The white Southerner is subject to the same set of social mandates out of which he creates "nigger," and he becomes himself a form of behavior. Any such rote adherence purely to form, as opposed to substantive concerns, operates to negate individual identity. Quentin functions almost solely in relation to traditional forms of behavior. He seems unaware that Deacon, in his public posturing, his uniforms and manners, reflects Quentin's own movement in a behavioral pattern that is equally as stylized, if less flagrant.

Neither does Quentin read himself into Deacon's observation, " 'I draw no petty social lines. A man is to me a man, wherever I find him.' " Quentin does draw such lines; even in his search for Deacon, he does not see that a man is a man. But Deacon seems to intimate that there is indeed a possibility for Quentin to become a man; for certainly Deacon accepts Quentin in much the same way as does Louis Hatcher, a black farmer in Mississippi, who accepts Quentin as a hunter—a member of the fraternity of virile Southern men.

Louis Hatcher, like Deacon, is a man prepared for living. In a comic scene that has serious resonances for Deacon's meeting with Quentin, Louis attributes his survival of a devasting flood to cleaning his lantern and keeping it ready. Quentin responds to the story in disbelief, but he receives a serious answer from a black perspective: " 'Yes, suh. You do you way en I do mine.' " Louis is a poor, uneducated black man, who has achieved a certain prepared "light" in his existence. In cleaning his lamp, Louis has prepared for living, even if living is dangerous. He knows how to adapt, to survive with dignity and grace. He displays a personal integration of self and harmony with the world, as his clear, mellow voice ("a part of darkness and silence, coiling out of it, coiling into it again") and his ever-ready lantern suggest. Louis is akin to Deacon and the Gibsons; their lives are as resilient as Louis's voice. But, Louis Hatcher, like Deacon and the Gibsons, is black, and his model for living is incomprehensible to the white youth, who cannot recognize those pragmatic elements in blacks that would be useful guides for his choosing life over death.

Quentin, because he is so out of touch with self and world, does not see the disparity between his actions and reality, though he can spot obvious contradictions in others. For example, he reflects, specifically on the question of southerners' awareness of "niggers" in the North: "I learned that the best way to take all people, black or white, is to take them for what they think they are, then leave them alone." But Quentin is unable to translate his words into positive action, particularly in terms of his family and his sister Caddy.

When Quentin takes a train back to the South during the Christmas holidays, he has an experience that allows for the expression of the sentiment underlying his relationship with Deacon. After the train has stopped in Virginia, Quentin looks out the window and sees: "a nigger on a mule in the middle of the stiff ruts, waiting for the train to move. . . . he sat straddle of the mule his head wrapped in a piece of blanket, as if they had been built there with the fence and the road, or with the hill, carved of the hill itself, like a sign put there saying You are home again." The single image of the black man at home in the southern landscape carries Quentin's thoughts to the familiar environs of Jefferson and home as no other single figure or impression could have. A Negro on a mule is a traditional figure extending backwards into the southern past, and it is a recurring image from Faulkner's first novel.

Immediately Quentin begins to act out a ritual exchange with the man on the mule by playing "Christmas gift." The man's ready response, " 'Sho comin, boss. You done caught me, aint you?' " asserts what is for Quentin the natural order of things. Both know from habit, and perhaps instinct, what the ritual entails:

> "I'll let you off this time." I dragged my pants out of the little hammock and got a quarter out. "But look out next time. I'll be coming back here two days after New Year, and look out then." I threw the quarter out the window. "Buy yourself some Santy Claus."
>
> "Yes, suh," he said. He got down and picked up the quarter and rubbed it on his leg. "Thanky, young marster. Thanky."

Quentin feels a need for the game and encourages the mechanical participation of the black man, because it confirms for him the reality of traditional relationships.

This incident is comparable to Mrs. Bland's telling "how Gerald throws his nigger downstairs and how the nigger plead to be allowed to matriculate in the divinity school to be near marster marse gerald and How he ran all the way to the station beside the carriage with tears in his eyes when marse gerald rid away." The two incidents reveal the tendency of distorted perceptions to exaggerate the meaning of the Negro to suit an image of the aristocratic master, gallantly inspiring devotion. "Quentin attempts," Olga Vickery maintains, "to coerce experience into conformity with his system" (*The Novels of William Faulkner*). He sees himself as a gentleman of the Old South, and the Negro functions in accordance with his preconceptions. Mrs. Bland's story of Gerald's Negro is only a more extreme example of the same phenomenon. Neither Mrs. Bland nor Quentin sees the Negro as a person, and in reenacting rigid conventions, neither allows for individual self-development.

Ultimately, the meaning that Quentin distills from the Christmas gift incident is predictably disappointing, especially if he is to be considered a perceptive, sensitive youth:

> I leaned out the window . . . looking back. He stood there beside the gaunt rabbit of a mule, the two of them shabby and motionless and unimpatient. . . . they passed smoothly from sight that way, with that quality about them of shabby and timeless patience, of static serenity: that blending of childlike and ready incompetence and paradoxical reliability that tends and protects them it loves out of all reason and robs them steadily and evades responsibility and obligations by means too barefaced to be called subterfuge even and is taken in theft or evasion with only that frank and spontaneous admiration for the victor which a gentleman feels for anyone who beats him in a fair contest, and withal a fond and unflagging tolerance for white folks' vagaries like that of a grandparent for unpredictable and troublesome children, which I had forgotten.

The Negro and mule standing "motionless and unimpatient" is a metaphor characterizing Jefferson and home, the way Quentin would like them to be. This scene of "static serenity" provides Quentin with a comforting image of a familiar, fixed world. The existence of man and mule confirms the reality of Quentin's sense of home. If "the greatest enemy of Quentin's ethical system is time," then the Negro on the mule is reassuring because of his timelessness. Poised in a substantial, enduring natural setting, he is the age-old conception of the South's "nigger." Frozen with his mule into a portrait simultaneously then and now, the Negro is literally the closest the southerner can come to a tangible configuration of continuity and permanence.

Quentin's thoughts, however, evidence a duality that is not simply a matter of praising the Negro in spite of his shortcoming; it appears more to be a praising him for faults which magnify the white man's difference and assure him of a special place in his world. His thinking about the Negro relieves the pressure of evaluating his family, home, and himself as they exist in actuality. Quentin's experience of life is shallow and his thoughts reflect as much. Richard P. Adams aptly terms this passage a "collection of condescending clichés" (*Faulkner: Myth and Motion*). These clichés expose Quentin's inability to work imaginatively within a given context of human interaction, as well as his lack of creative images or ideas. They reveal that his emotional and psychological dilemma will go unresolved. He may have an artist's sensibilities, but he is an extremely sterile and derivative artist. His thoughts disclose a mind that is already dead, smothered by a tradition in which he wholeheartedly believes.

In Quentin's monologue, Faulkner experiments with a more complex method of incorporating the Negro into his fiction. He mirrors and manifests the white youth's fragmentation by means of a subtle handling of the Negro's presence in a divided world. His strategy involves the larger metaphorical value of the Negro. He uses Deacon and the other blacks literally and figuratively to delineate an illusive reality and to render emotional stasis. His method, a symbolic extension of the relationship between the Gibsons and Compsons, widens the juxtaposition of blacks and whites to include sympathetic and antagonistic psychological relationships. Although in this section, and in the novel as a whole, Faulkner implies but does not fully develop the antagonism between the races, he seems much more aware of its literary potential, particularly in his use of Deacon to delineate Quentin's cultural conditioning as a cause of mental stress and psychical division.

Faulkner's method of handling blacks is similar to an observation Quentin makes about blacks coming "into white people's lives . . . in sudden sharp black trickles that isolate white facts for an instant in unarguable truth like under a microscope; the rest of the time [blacks are] just voices that laugh when you see nothing to laugh at, tears when no reason for tears." Quentin perceives two separate realities for whites and blacks; his "white facts," for example, assume black facts as a corollary, an assumption which Faulkner uses for making ideological distinctions between his fictional worlds. Whereas Quentin observes that blacks penetrate white consciousness suddenly and thereafter have no discernible meaning for whites, Faulkner utilizes blacks to illuminate or magnify aspects of his white characters and afterwards confines them to the background as an actual or symbolic presence responding to a reality incomprehensible to whites.

The Discovery of Loss in *The Sound and the Fury*

John T. Matthews

Though Faulkner told several versions of the genesis of *The Sound and the Fury,* in nearly all of them he explained Benjy as less a character than a way of seeing grief. Faulkner remarked to Jean Stein:

> You can't feel anything for Benjy because he doesn't feel any-thing. He was a prologue. . . . He serves his purpose and is gone. . . . He recognizes tenderness and love though he could not have named them, and it was the threat to tenderness and love that caused him to bellow when he felt the change in Caddy. He no longer had Caddy; being an idiot he was not even aware that Caddy was missing. He knew only that something was wrong, which left a vacuum in which he grieved. He tried to fill that vacuum.

In Nagano, Faulkner identified Benjy with "the idea of the blind, self-centeredness of innocence, typified by children, if one of those children had been truly innocent, that is, an idiot." The predicament of loss and articu-lation also governs Faulkner's reading of the dilemmas of the other Comp-son brothers and the narrator in section 4. Beginning with Benjy's, each section broods on how to "fill that vacuum." Can memory or speech successfully reappropriate the natural presence of Caddy, whose absence initiates the discourse? To recover Caddy would be to restore full natural significance to the world. Each brother denies, at the same time that his section reveals, that memory is supplementary, like a kind of writing. Benjy

---

From *The Play of Faulkner's Language.* © 1982 by Cornell University Press.

and Quentin are doomed to reappropriate nothing except Caddy as already disappearing; she is, in their sections, already the trace that is an origin, and her absolute plenitude can never be evoked in their minds. A permutation of this pattern carries us into Jason's section, for he has apparently satisfied himself with an elaborate financial compensation for the inaccessibilty of Caddy. Yet his incessant frustration feeds on the necessary failure of the supplement to recover the thing itself. The unresolvable contradictions of each brother's vision ripen in the last section into the rich paradoxes of Faulkner's mature fiction. The novel, as it approaches its cessation, wins the recognition that articulation can never "fill the vacuum," but only create within it; that it can never successfully convert the original image of Caddy's muddy drawers suspended in the tree into a finished story; and that it may luxuriate precisely in the endlessness of the task.

Benjy is the neccessary prologue because his agony is literally the dumbshow of the novel's crises. If his idiocy is the formal arresting of childhood, it is because the infant-man registers loss purely, manipulates the simplest expressions of that loss grotesquely, can never know the more consoling, more dangerous powers of speech, and is locked in a section that mirrors rhetorically—in its simple style and narrative voicelessness—his impotence to grieve well.

The Sound and the Fury opens to a disequilibrium already accomplished. The double movement of the opening passages is Luster's "hunting" for his lost quarter and Benjy's incomprehending search for something that the word "caddie" reminds him of. As we subsequently learn, of course, his sister's disappearance eighteen years earlier has tipped the child into the fallen world of loss, memory, time, and grief. In the interval, Benjy remains perfectly arrested on this threshold, surrounded by signs of Caddy's absence. According to Henri Bergson, the primary activity of the mind as it encounters pure duration (which "might well be nothing but a succession of qualitative changes . . . pure heterogeneity) is to spatialize (*Time and Free Will*, trans. F. L. Pogson). The mind converts time into space as it conceptualizes, imposes images, and finally "solidif[ies] our impressions in order to express them in language." Benjy's pertinence to Faulkner's deep exploration of the nature of articulation in *The Sound and the Fury* begins with this impulse to translate raw change into a kind of topo[s]graphic stability.

One consequence of this activity is that the Compson grounds become a simple analogue for the memory. Every site of Benjy's domain opens immediate access to all of the moments that have ever occured there: to duck through the "broken place" in the fence with Luster in 1928 is to emerge with Caddy two decades earlier. The garden gate, the fence along the pasture, the "graveyard" on the lawn, and so on, all have their special associations. Physical location must serve in the mind of this truly innocent child for topos of an idea, image, or word. Once Caddy has vanished, Benjy's constrained memory cannot sufficiently recall her (the Appendix affirms that he "could not remember his sister but only the loss of her"); the formal equivalent of his bondage to tangible reminders of his sister is his physical confinement (" 'Yes sir.' Versh said. 'We dont never let him get off the place' ").

Discussion of *The Sound and the Fury* has well established that Benjy primitively stabilizes his world by hoarding relics of Caddy after she leaves. Olga Vickery refers to the process of "mechanical identification" that designates the slipper, the spot where the mirror once hung, the smell of trees, the jimson weed in the bottle, and so on as things whose presence partially fills the void left by Caddy. Benjy's spatialization of loss succeeds in his strictly sensual realm; he needs objects to see and to fondle, objects that above all must be *there*. Luster can always torment him by duplicating the process of dispossession: when he hides Benjy's flowers "they went away. I began to cry. . . . The flowers came back. . . . 'Hush.' Luster said. 'Here they is. Look. It's fixed back just like it was at first. Hush, now.' " Of course, Benjy's collection of sacred relics has evident symbolic logic for the reader; for example, the mirror, which Benjy also senses is some kind of door may suggest the narcissistic essence of sibling love and incest; or the jimson weed may be appropriate because of its phallic associations. But Benjy's selection of certain objects also has an internal logic that deserves attention because it enriches the crisis of articulation that Benjy himself experiences and initiates for the novel.

One of the more moving portions of Derrida's *Of Grammatology* rehearses a moment in Rousseau's *Essay* that imagines the intrusion of gesture into the immediacy of love. Rousseau believes that love invents the gesture of drawing: "How she could say things to her beloved, who traced his shadow with such pleasure! What sounds might she use to render this movement of the magic wand?" The drawing and speaking constitute primal articulation—an effort to signify *within* the movement of full pleasure and presence. Derrida systematically uncovers Rousseau's own confession of the impossibility of such simultaneity, and yet, for the moment, he recapitulates Rousseau with tenderness:

> The movement of the magic wand that traces with so much pleasure does not fall outside of the body. Unlike the spoken or written sign, it does not cut itself off from the desiring body of

the person who traces or from the immediately perceived image of the other. It is of course still an image which is traced at the tip of the wand, but an image that is not completely separated from the person it represents; what the drawing draws is almost present in person in his *shadow*. The distance from the shadow or from the wand is almost nothing. She who traces, holding, handling, now the wand, is very close to touching what is very close to being the other *itself*, close by a minute difference; that small difference—visibility, spacing, death—is undoubtedly the origin of the sign and the breaking of immediacy.

Benjy's heart fixes on some of the objects in his collection precisely because they are just barely separated from the body of the beloved. The "minute difference," the tiniest of gaps, separates Caddy from her slipper. What she has worn has been quite nearly her body itself, and now Benjy seizes the article that encased an extremity, as if detaching the garment from the foot constitutes the very passage from the other itself to that which "is very close to being the other itself." A similar impulse accounts for Benjy's infatuation with firelight. From the standpoint of the novel's thematics, of course, Caddy's association with fire in Benjy's naive memory connotes her passion and affection; but Benjy himself notes that when Caddy sat before the hearth, her "hair was like fire, and little points of fire were in her eyes." Benjy unthinkingly preserves the substance that has helped him to describe (or draw) her body for him. In her absence, Caddy also "becomes" the fragrance of trees; such an association extends the principle of selection at work here, for an odor is both part of and already minutely different from the body itself. It seems to linger and hover between absolute presence and absence. Benjy remembers the mirror (which by 1928 has faded into a dark spot on the wall) for similar reasons. The figures of childhood pass into a not quite present, not quite absent state when they appear in the mirror: "we could see Caddy fighting in the mirror and father put me down and went into the mirror and fought too. . . . Father brought Caddy to the fire. They were all out of the mirror." The mirror is the spot where "visibility, spacing, death" signify the "breaking of immediacy."

Benjy, who has barely emerged into time, responds to loss with the barest of articulations. And yet the time "which shadows every mans brow even Benjy's" (as Mr. Compson later puts it) presents dead spaces in the very core of Benjy's relics. The objects can neither substitute fully for Caddy nor reappropriate her presence; they derive meaning only as they embody Caddy as already dying from the plenitude of full presence. The firelight "contains" Caddy, but when Benjy reaches into it to regain her, he burns his hand in its alien, destructive difference. Similarly, Benjy associate the fragrance of trees contradictorily—both with Caddy's virginal innocence and with the onset of her sexual betrayal. That she always "smelled like trees" makes the paradox of natural innocence and natural maturation sensible to Benjy's nostrils; at the heart of his memory of her full presence is already the trace of her disappearance. And when Caddy steps into the mirror she does so to fight—to flee the mirror herself or to drive another out of it. Derrida's discussion of the trace at the origin and of the inescapable deathliness of the supplement refreshes our conception of how Benjy's fumbling attempts to neutralize grief initiate the crisis of articulation that informs the novel.

Once Benjy commits himself to filling the vacuum, in fact, he has fully ceded Caddy to the difference of signs. Accordingly, some of his mementoes become much more arbitrary designates of loss: the jimson weed, its bottle, and the narcissus are—for all the symbolic properties apparent to us—unmotivated signs for Benjy. They have no intrinsic meaning. Curiously, this arbitrary substitution of one presence for a first, more natural presence stands at the implicit center of *The Sound and the Fury*. It is a commonplace in psychological discussions of the novel to identify Mrs. Compson's coldness and inaccessibility as the root of the brothers' diseased obsession with their sister, who accepts the mantle of surrogate maternity. But we might also consider Mrs. Compson herself as a shadow of whatever the absolute plenitude would have been. For Derrida, such a site cannot exist, for as soon as it has been signified it is no longer: at the absolute origin one finds only the architrace. To the extent that *The Sound and the Fury* is about the relationship between the felt loss of plenitude and the necessity to substitute, we might describe Caddy's role in the novel as the architrace. She is herself, that is, a supplement. For Derrida's Rousseau, "presence, always natural, which for Rousseau more than for others means maternal, *ought to be* self-sufficient." Therefore, Rousseau can recognize supplementarity only as dangerous. Likewise, Caddy replaces her mother (who fails to embody maternal fullness) and becomes the dangerous supplement, the necessary addition to what should have been self-sufficient. Benjy, like his brothers, sought his mother but found his sister. After Mrs. Compson pities her "poor baby" idiot son, Caddy objects: " 'You're not a poor baby. Are you. You've got your Caddy.' " The supplement's wealth enriches the dispossessed child.

The articulated shapes of loss, those sites and objects that embody the "visibility, spacing, death" that Derrida finds at the "origin" of the sign, provide tenuous peace for Benjy. They are variations of the "smooth, bright shapes" that lull Benjy into the relative calm of having forgotten Caddy and remembering only her loss, as the passage I quoted earlier from the Appendix puts it. The configuration of loss, indeed, governs virtually every detail of Benjy's picturing of the past. The scenes that populate his memory emerge only because they present a Caddy who is already dying to Benjy. André Bleikasten correctly notices that "most scenes in which [Benjy] is directly implicated are scenes of dispossession" and that death permeates the episodes that he remembers. But Benjy also blindly struggles with a paradox of memory: the Caddy he wishes to remember can be recalled only when her absence is absolute. Memory, speech, and desire depend on the unavailability of their object. Remarkably, Benjy's memories of Caddy embody the paradox since they cannot represent her except as beginning to disappear. Her first appearance in his section occurs at the point of a breach: crawling through the fence's broken place, Caddy guides their exit from the grounds. Moreover, she has been sent by Uncle Maury to deliver instructions for his assignation with a neighbor; thus even in childhood she is the agent of sexual license and treachery, and ultimately will suffer exile from the garden. (And, in bearing a written message, she signals the burden she accepts throughout the novel as a word-laden escapee.) The conflation of Damuddy's funeral, Caddy's muddying, the wedding, and Mr. Compson's funeral confirms the fact that Caddy can be remembered only as already contaminated by the process of change and impending absence. So far as I can tell, Benjy never remembers a moment of untroubled, blissful intimacy with Caddy. When he hugs her it is mutely to protest her infidelities; when she cradles him in bed, he can register only that first she has stayed away or that she keeps her bathrobe on for the first time. The discourse of Benjy's memory conforms to Derrida's definition of the supplement as that which both recognizes its difference and defers the (impossible) reappropriation of presence. Benjy's rudimentary version of these difficulties opens the way to Faulkner's deepest commitment to renouncing the illusion of natural presence and accepting the ecstasy of writing.

Benjy is a grotesque born of an experiment. The true innocence of this child resides—as Faulkner suggested in the comments I quoted at the beginning of the chapter—in his inability to name his grief. Benjy can produce sound but cannot mark it; moaning and bellowing place him eternally on the threshold of speech. The vision of loss without the power of utterance is the opening cut of the novel. Caddy summarizes succinctly as the hands of dispossession encircle her:

"No, no," Caddy said. "No. No."

"He can't talk." Charlie said. "Caddy."

"Are you crazy." Caddy said. She began to breathe fast. "He can see. Dont."

The pulse of Benjy's section is disturbance and placation. Every loss that he suffers—whether it is Caddy disappearing into marriage or merely his flower being snatched away by Luster—must be met with some effort to "fix [it] back again just like it was at first." Benjy's mute arrangement of relics and his dumbshow of protest whenever Caddy threatened to leave in childhood suggest the nature of his innocent articulation. That he cannot actually "talk" does not exclude him from primitive efforts of speech, however. When Caddy applies her perfume, Benjy moans at her betrayal ("So that was it. And you were trying to tell Caddy and you couldn't tell her"). When he passes the gate and assaults the Burgess girl, he is reaching out to repossess Caddy. Long after Caddy's school days, three years after her marriage, Benjy faithfully awaits his sister's return from absence. The little girl who comes into view is momentarily given significance in Benjy's silent speech:

> They came on. I opened the gate and they stopped, turning. I was trying to say, and I caught her, trying to say, and she screamed and I was trying to say and trying and the bright shapes began to stop and I tried to get out.

The conflation of Benjy's "trying to say" and his sexual assault on the Burgess girl leads us back to the connection between desire and speech. Benjy's verbal and sexual impotences keep him from intercourses that would more nearly figure reunion with Caddy. Benjy's assault and punitive castration epitomize his imprisonment in the infancy of the imagination. His clutching at the little girl and his howls of depossession are both clumsy burlesques of the other brothers' (and the whole novel's) attempts to recover and relate, to touch and tell. Quentin likewise finds himself powerless to engage either some other female or the remembered past so as to transform and replace Caddy. Faulkner, as I shall discuss shortly, thoroughly grasps both the accomplishments and dangers of the word as the novel unfolds the crisis of articulation. As for Benjy, the time that captures Caddy and creates his sense of loss cannot be mastered by his brute voice: "I could still hear the clock between my voice."

To the extent that criticism of *The Sound and the Fury* has been willing to recognize "authorial" interests in each of the sections, it has suggested that the Compson brothers' and Dilsey's difficulties in dealing with loss reflect the novelist's familiar frustrations with language. Bleikasten, for example, is surely right in reading Benjy's "trying to say" as a motto for the troubled efforts of the novel to articulate its own meaning. I wish to argue, however, that a conflicting urgency fills out what is for Faulkner a paradox of the word: the inability of language fully to embody the absolute, the lost origin, becomes the happy resource of the prolonged life of speech. I think that this argument might expose areas of contact between Faulkner and the protagonists of *The Sound and the Fury* that have not been sufficiently thought about. For example, Benjy's inescapable muteness confers a kind of tranquillity and order that a novelist might dream about and then forswear in order to write.

Despite the prevailing mood of barely eased agony in the first section, Benjy has managed to stabilize his world. His terrible muteness—although it prevents a nameable knowledge of his loss—paradoxically blesses Benjy with serenity. Precisely because he has forgotten Caddy and can remember only her loss, the pitiful collection of relics can placate him. As an individual, Caddy has disappeared into the signs that Benjy substitutes for her. By clutching to himself these things that are just barely different from Caddy herself, Benjy arrests processive dispossession: Caddy is never closer to returning in our eyes, but she is never any father away in Benjy's. There are two aspects to Benjy's "successful" silence, then: Caddy has been frozen by the objects associated with her and can never be any "more absent" than she is, and Benjy's grief can grow neither greater nor smaller. Unlike Quentin, who relies entirely on his memories of his sister, Benjy need not worry that someday his grief will be less painful. He cannot give his agony away fully to the deadening, distancing properties of language.

That Benjy intuits the deadly properties of the word may be seen in his reaction to the utterance of his sister's name. Unlike his handful of tangible mementoes, the word "Caddy" is a terrifying representative of the absent one. From the opening lines of the novel we learn the unique word that will set Benjy howling. So violent a reflex may suggest the powerfully threatening magic of the uttered word. To begin with, the word flirts with intimate knowledge. Benjy's howls never incarnate a version of Caddy, and so he never enjoys the illusion of reappropriation that language allows. Since he cannot formulate Caddy as word, he forgets her and remembers only her loss. To name is to know; later in the novel, when hunger arouses Ben's whimpering, it is "hunger itself inarticulate, not knowing it is hunger." In addition, the spoken word seems to mediate presence and absence more profoundly than other signs: the name magically seems part of the presence itself. A name may summon (when she was a child, to call Caddy was to have her); the name is the owner's most intimate possession (Caddy uses her name consistently when she talks to Benjy about herself in the third person); the uttered name is a tactile presence (evoking the absent one) which is also an absence (it disappears into the hearer). And the spoken word even reproduces the rhythm of possession and dispossession as it is spoken and then fades from audibility: speech itself becomes a kind of dispossession. One's words fall from the mouth and are "stolen" as others receive them. Benjy, like Quentin and Jason, guards against such a second theft. Moreover, the acoustic sign for Caddy only intensifies the general dilemma; that which is most proper to Caddy, her name, is also least the property of her person. The name outrages Benjy by speaking in her absence.

From this point of view I hope to see how the novel takes quite seriously the prohibitions against language in the opening sections. The novel fears the realizations of two opposing and equally impossible dreams: on the one hand, a pure silence beckons as the realm of unarticulated representation, a place where immediacy has never been broken. Benjy's and Quentin's memories strive, unavailingly, to exorcise the curse of mediacy from their imaginations of the past. But what they remember is already clouded by deathliness and forgetfulness, as we have begun to see. On the other hand, the novel as a whole makes acrobatic efforts to tell its whole story fully—to "get it right." The nature of language, Faulkner comes to suggest, forbids the illusion that any original idea, image, or sense can be embodied in words. Instead, *The Sound and the Fury* discovers, the fun of writing is in the play of failures, in the incompleteness, deferment, and repeatability of texts. The fiction veers away from resolution and completion in order to prolong its life. Accordingly, the novel makes two sorts of gesture toward silence, one toward the refusal to speak, the other toward deliberate mutations of the narrative's self-satisfaction.

A most arresting consequence of the paradox of silent speech in *The Sound and the Fury* is the mode of the novel. The stream-of-consciousness "monologues" accomplish more than the simple trick of simulating the immediacy of mental processes. They succeed, as well, in effacing any presumed narrator. In effect, they formally respond to the aspiration of writing a novel that is beyond the usual constraints of language. Gerard Genette's *Discours du récit* (in *Figures III*) may provide a vocabulary for our discussion. The *mode* of a work of fiction may be determined by attention to two aspects: distance and perspective. Distance governs the proximity of the "actual" events to the occasion or scene of their recounting. Perspective is the point of view from which these events are seen. The question of "Qui voit?," however, is separate from the question of "Qui parle?" The latter opens a consideration of the *voice* of the novel, as opposed to its mode. If we apply Genette's further discriminations within these categories, we may arrive at a deeper understanding of *The Sound and the Fury*'s rhetoric of silence. For we can easily decide that the monologues of *The Sound and the Fury* are examples of what Genette calls *discours immediat,* with no apparent distance between the events of April 7, 1928, and their recitation. Moreover, Benjy's perspective rules his section (as each protagonist's does in the subsequent two sections). Yet we cannot successfully address the problem of a speaking voice in the opening sections because they deliberately both imply and deny the presence of a narrator's voice. Despite the first-person voice, Benjy surely cannot be speaking in his section as an interior monologue (the situation is multiplied in *As I Lay Dying*); but neither can we posit even an impersonal narrator recounting Benjy's impressions on some timeless occasion of the novel's telling. Rather, the section emerges as a text intent on masquerading as a state of mind. The act of narration effaces itself in the mode and voice of the early stream-of-consciousness sections of the novel. The monologues simply appear as written discourse, issuing from no voice or hand. Such a strategy marks Faulkner's discovery of the space of writing—outside the boundaries of personal presence or presumed consciousness.

Some familiar aspects of the style of Benjy's section endorse the impression that this first telling of the story is an artificially circumscribed, or partially silenced, performance. We recognize, for example, the preponderance of simple sentence structure and the actual repetition of many sentences. Benjy's sensations, like the sentences that render them, produce only the bluntest discriminations: when he registers Caddy's presence it is because "Caddy smelled like trees," a sentence that recurs frequently. The fondness of the style in this section for particular phrases and images sympathetically imitates Benjy's fondness for familiar objects and sites. Once the discourse has surveyed Benjy's world, it does not compel the narrative to advance. Style elaborates and expands Benjy's world, but it does not increasingly deepen or unfold it.

A related inertness in the style records Benjy's dependence on the senses, particularly his sight. His section is crowded with prepositions that perpetually strive to locate experience in a static visual array. ("Through the fence, between the curling flower spaces, I could see them hitting," the novel begins.) Moreover, the language of his mind is inhospitable to anything except the simplest pictures: "They were hitting little, across the pasture. I went back along the fence to where the flag was. It flapped on the bright grass and the trees." In the preceding sentence we may notice that an adjective ("little") usurps an adverb's place, draining the verb of its energy and slowing it into a picture; and the flag flapping "on" the grass and trees suggest the superimposition of foreground on background.

As Benjy reckons with his loss through primitive forms of articulation, so his section reflects the difficulties with which a novel begins to fashion its meaning. The imagery and allusive symbolism that eventually accrete significance as they recur through the novel are presented "innocently" in Benjy's discourse. The true innocence of the infant's mind permits us a glimpse into the process by which the structures of a work grow into a kind of authority from arbitrary origins. The opening section serves as a primer for the novel's education in articulation.

The gesture of defining and naming permeates Benjy's eternal childhood. Caddy, for example, recognizes that one of her responsibilities is to teach Benjy the words for things. Stopping at the branch on the way to the Pattersons', Caddy scoops a piece of ice to show Benjy: " 'Ice. That means how cold it is.' " Death, Caddy, explains to her brothers, is " 'when Nancy fell in the ditch and Roskus shot her and the buzzards came and undressed her." Frony, likewise, offers the definition of a funeral:

> "What's a funeral." Jason said. . . .
> "Where they moans." Frony said.

At one point Caddy herself needs information, which her older brother supplies: " 'When is the Lawd's own time, Dilsey.' Caddy said. 'It's Sunday.' Quentin said." Occasions of definition in the first section make a figure of the act of naming, and that figure may be noticed in other levels of discourse. In addition, these definitions happen to share the theme of death: Caddy's running out of childhood into adulthood epitomizes the processes of cooling, disrobing, and mourning which contribute to the thematic and symbolic essence of *The Sound and the Fury*.

Throughout Benjy's section images and episodes struggle to present themselves as potentially significant. The process resembles the literal acts of naming by equipping the reader with a lexicon that promises eventual fluency in the novel's terms of discourse. For example, we notice Benjy's infatuation with Caddy's veil at her wedding: "*Then I saw Caddy, with flowers in her hair, and a long veil like shining wind. Caddy Caddy.*" Only Quentin's poetic associations convert the veil from image to symbol, however. To him the veil screens him from his mirrored image (the narcissism that is his incest); it muffles the voice of childhood's Eden; it signifies the shadow of time and death:

> Running out of the mirror the smell roses roses the voice that breathed o'er Eden. Then she was across the porch I couldn't hear her heels then in the moonlight like a cloud, the floating shadow of the veil running across the grass, into the bellowing. She ran out of her dress, clutching the bridal. . . . Shreve said, "Well. . . .Is it a wedding or a wake?"

In Quentin's section the veil becomes the marriage adornment and the funeral shroud — the barrier to repossession. Benjy's innocent eyes can see none of this. Similarly, the section naively introduces the tree-climbing episode and the image of the muddy drawers. To Benjy they mean nothing:

> He went and pushed Caddy up into the tree to the first limb. We watched the muddy bottom of her drawers. Then we couldn't see her.
>
> "Just look at you." Dilsey said. She wadded the drawers and scrubbed Caddy behind with them. "It done soaked clean through onto you." she said. "But you wont get no bath this night."

But Quentin's preoccupation with sexuality, filth, and morality subsequently gives these lines impressive prophetic implications, since Caddy's literal undressing becomes (as Caddy's description of Nancy's death hints) the prefiguration of her death to her brothers. And Dilsey's "It done soaked clean through onto you" must be read as marking the end of a childhood. What we find throughout Benjy's section—in the mode, voice, style, imagery—is only the rudimentary articulation.

For the novel as a whole we might want to think of these common processes of initial definition as prefiguration, the naming of gestures and images that will be repeated as governing structures. It is prefiguration only in a limited sense, however, for the novel steadfastly avoids developing any fully coherent system of meaning. No single telling can ever get its part of the story "right" or final; instead, the novel increasingly incites the play of meaning. The supplement can never eradicate its "difference." While veils, shadows, and so on may be important to Benjy's and Quentin's sections, wholly different symbolic economies govern Jason's mind. There are certainly points of contact among the sections, but the prevailing impression among readers is probably represented by Donald Kartiganer's sensible discussion of the separately clarified visions of each section. Perhaps the status of the allusions to Christianity best exemplifies the novel's manner. As is well known, Benjy's section introduces the comparison of Caddy to Eve; Caddy climbs the pear tree (later confused with an apple tree in Faulkner's memory), consorts with snakes, disobeys her "paw's" command to stay out of the tree, and is once called "Satan" by Dilsey. And yet, like the Passion Week structure with which it harmonizes, the Fall paradigm coheres fully neither within Benjy's section nor within the novel as a whole. The pattern satisfies momentary discursive needs as it evokes the fall into sexual differentiation for Benjy and Quentin, or reminds us, perhaps, of the deceit of the devil's tongue, but Faulkner forestalls the emergence of any fully intelligible analogues in *The Sound and the Fury*. (Contrast the meticulous model of *A Fable*.) I have been suggesting that such a forestalling reflects both the impossibility of the supplement (Benjy's memory and the written novel) to reappropriate presence and the recognition that such a limitation opens the possibility of the endless pleasures of writing. Benjy's mind constitutes the most natural, primitive activity of articulation. His serenity is predicated on a kind of speech. As the novel's closing words intone, "his eyes were empty and blue and serene again as cornice and facade flowed smoothly once more from left to right; post and tree, window and doorway, and signboard, each in its ordered place." The signboards replace the absent Caddy even as they differ from the original plenitude. Similarly, the deep resources of narrative as supplement are barely tapped in the first section. The novel must accustom itself to its own activity: submerged in an idiot's mind, the narrative voice effaces itself; confronted by tumultuous change, the style repeats itself; deprived of assertion, the symbolism can only insinuate and forecast.

II

The Sound and the Fury leaves Benjy on the threshold of expression, groping innocently to "fill that vacuum" of Caddy's loss with mute speech. Unlike his brother, Quentin has perfect license to engage his formidable memory, imagination, and eloquence in the task of articulating a response to loss. And yet his suicide expresses a refusal to accept the conditions and consequences of filling the vacuum. Since Sartre's fine early essay, criticism has fruitfully discussed the disappearance of Caddy as the precipitating crisis of Quentin's warfare with time. The indulged tyranny of his obsession with the past, his notorious clock phobia, his preoccupation with virginity and imaginary incest, and his eventual suicide may all, of course, be read as desperate gambits to deny Caddy's loss and to reappropriate her presence.

In Derrida's term, Quentin wants to reappropriate a lost plenitude. What has not been studied carefully about Quentin's mind is his horror at having to regain Caddy through a mere simulacrum of her "original" presence. Although he is equipped to invent substitutions for the absent Caddy, Quentin recoils from the intuition that even memory is a kind of supplement that arises out of the breakage of immediacy, that necessarily acknowledges "visibility, spacing, death."

As it does for Benjy, Caddy's loss seems to constitute time's destruction of childhood's absolute and innocent love for Quentin. We are familiar with Quentin's capacity to explain the disturbance of his world abstractly; Caddy's sexual maturation—her lost virginity—becomes the apparent synecdoche of the universal process of time: "When the shadow of the sash appeared on the curtains it was between seven and eight oclock and then I was in time again, hearing the watch," Quentin's section begins. Time is indisputably Quentin's antagonist because it has stolen Caddy, but it is equally responsible in Quentin's mind for a second threat, one that has not always been attended to. Quentin seeks desperately to devote his memory to the rites of commemoration, to neutralize Caddy's loss by occupying himself solely with memories of her. But time weakens memory itself, as Mr. Compson's voice insists:

> and i temporary and he you cannot bear to think that someday
> it will no longer hurt you like this now were getting at it.

The danger that so paralyzes Quentin is not that the past will overcome the present, as Sartre and others have argued, but that the present will extinguish the possibility of remembering the past. Faulkner's own conviction that "was" cannot exist because if it did there would be no grief helps to point up Quentin's crisis. His private vision of half-imagined, half-remembered incest aspires "to isolate [Caddy] out of the loud world so that it would have to flee us of necessity"; it is a vision consecrated to recovering the fullness of love and meaning that Caddy's absolute presence now seems to have constituted. If his memory fails to hold on to Caddy, Quentin risks the annihilation of sense, identity, continuity. In moments of despairing anguish Quentin glimpses a past denuded of Caddy's focal power:

> until after the honeysuckle got all mixed up in it the whole thing
> came to symbolise night and unrest I seemed to be lying neither
> asleep nor awake looking down a long corridor of grey half-
> light where all stable things had become shadowy paradoxical
> all I had done shadows all I had felt suffered taking visible form
> antic and perverse mocking without relevance inherent them-

selves with the denial of the significance they should have affirmed thinking I was I was not who was not was not who.

By inciting his memories of Caddy from childhood to invade the present,
Quentin temporarily fights off this world of meaninglessness. Caddy is
Quentin's decreed center of inherent or natural significance, the base of
stability, the core of original identity. Quentin's memory seeks to retain
this center (or to reappropriate its presence.)

The underlying irony—and it is paradigmatic of Quentin's dilemma—
is that Caddy could never have been an original source of significance or
plenitude. As we have noted in Benjy's section, Caddy's importance to her
brothers springs from Mrs. Compson's premature retirement. Withholding
herself from her sons, the mother forces them to find nurture and affection
in their sister. Methods of psychoanalysis offer the readiest explanations of
what such a substitution might mean, but we may also consider Caddy's
status in the context of the problems of loss and articulation. Once Quentin
has reached his last day and Caddy is dead to him, the oldest Compson
son confesses a prior absence: "if I'd just had a mother so I could say Mother
Mother." Quentin has no one to call mother and so his first act of articulation is to designate Caddy as substitute. I do not think it is overstating
the case to say that Quentin "supplements" Caroline Compson's insuf-
ficiency with Caddy. Dramatically, Caddy herself plays the role of the
supplement of the maternal presence; she appears as the trace at the origin,
the opening of expressible sense.

Because she is his sister, Caddy is a most "natural" supplement for
Quentin's mother. Both incestuous desire and its sanction have been trans-
fered across the tiniest of gaps; the ambivalences of the son toward the
mother may remain suspended in Quentin's attitudes toward Caddy. To
this extent Caddy indirectly reappropriates the forces of maternal presence.
Yet she also behaves according to her difference. Quentin cherishes Caddy's
virginity partially because it marks her pure maternity to him. Caddy is
the "mother" who has never been possessed by the son's father. Her lost
virginity signals to Quentin the loss of his substitute mother; he shrinks
from her pregnancy because it signals her literal (rather than functional)
motherhood. (Her daughter's name, Quentin, surely underscores the irony
of Caddy's treachery.) Caddy's virginity represents that impossible condition of absolute, original intactness that cannot be known until lost. Mr.
Compson instructs: "Women are never virgins. Purity is a negative state."
And in *Absalom* he amplifies: virginity "must depend upon its loss, absence,
to have existed at all."

That Quentin uses Caddy as a supplement may also be seen in the tension of their preadolescent attraction. What protects Caddy's virginity is, oddly enough, Quentin's incestuous love. Incest constitutes a limit of desire; it represents the necessary frustration of passion. Quentin never seeks possession of Caddy, for to do so would be to accept the supplement as a full presence in its own right, thereby destroying it. Instead, Quentin enjoys the deferring of passion enforced by the taboo against incest. He asks whether Caddy has not seen his face in those of her lovers, but he knows enough about the source of the supplement's life to reject the idea of actual sexual possession of his sister: "and he did you try to make her do it and i i was afraid to i was afraid she might and then it wouldnt have done any good." Caddy's value inheres in her unavailability, in the necessity of deferment. Herbert Head's caution to Caddy about her brother—"dont let Quentin do anything he cant finish"—may be less an insult than he supposes.

In one crucial respect, then, Quentin's behavior grows out of his conviction that Caddy once held the full presence of love and coherence and that her loss must be perfectly redeemed. The loss of the successful supplement resembles the sense of the lost origin. Because he does not confront the fact that Caddy is already a replacement, Quentin cannot imagine replacing her. Such an attitude betrays one of the components of Quentin's adolescent idiosyncrasies, and also helps to distinguish the larger attitudes of the novel toward this problem. For Quentin believes that time has turned presence into absence, while the novel—along with Faulkner's other mature fiction—seems to have won the recognition that there is never anything but the condition of already having lost. The state of diminishment or dispossession is the condition for articulation.

Quentin believes himself to be the victim of time. In addition to his celebrated combat with watches and clocks and his explicit meditation on the nature of time, Quentin remembers Caddy as being in dynamic synchronization with the natural time of sexual experimentation, pregnancy, and death. Caddy climbs the tree to see a funeral and earns Dilsey's affectionate diminutive "Minute" as a result. Caddy's "death" by sexual initiation is the very embodiment of human change, and of the division between the sexes that is the signature of a world fallen from atemporal unity. In the instant before his suicide Quentin remembers his father's intonation that "was[,] the saddest word of all," is the undeniable proof of man's misfortune, time. Mr. Compson accuses Quentin of seeking the "apotheosis" of a temporary state of mind because he cannot bear to think that his grief someday "will no longer hurt you like this." Against this sense of time as man's misfortune Quentin commits a memory devoted to saving Caddy herself. I protest that a discussion of articulation as supplement may enrich our understanding of this central, familiar issue in *The Sound and the Fury*. Quentin, unlike the novelist, refuses to accept language as loss because he identifies the supplementary nature of articulation as the death of the original plenitude. What he comes to intuit—and what makes his suicide so moving a creative gesture—is that even his hallowed memory deforms and substitutes for whatever was "there" at first.

Language is that potent instrument which articulates loss as soon as immediacy has broken. But Quentin deeply distrusts words because he recognizes what Rousseau might see as their necessary danger: they seek to recover what their very existence proclaims is no longer self-sufficient. Something of a nearly logophobic attitude connects Quentin's stray thoughts about language. His furious silence rejects the "loud world," which mistakenly believes that saying something will bring it about: "They all talked at once, their voices insistent and contradictory and impatient, making of unreality a possibility, then a probability, then an incontrovertible fact, as people will when their desires become words." Elsewhere he scornfully concedes that "people, using themselves and each other so much by words, are at least consistent in attributing wisdom to a still tongue." He abruptly cuts off the jeweler's inquiry about his attire with "This is just a private celebration" and prefers Roskus's "diffident, secret, inarticulate and sad" demeanor to Deacon's "long, pointless ancedotes." Silence guards Quentin's concentration on the lost Caddy. He risks no writing at all except notes whose posthumous delivery cannot jeopardize the vitality of his commemoration; and he will never contribute to the librarian's "shelves of ordered certitudes long divorced from reality, dessicating peacefully." The language of sexual difference already implicates Quentin in human discourse, but he once dreams of freedom from differentiation as if it would be an alien language: "It's not not having them. It's never to have had them then I could say O That That's Chinese I don't know Chinese."

Quentin avoids words because he senses that they displace and substitute, but he also identifies his silence as a failure of nerve. The refusal to speak ensures his imprisonment in the memory of the dead Caddy. A complaint about his own impotence appears in the lament I quoted earlier ("if I'd just had a mother so I could say Mother Mother"), as if saying Mother would have been the way to solve her loss. Earlier in this section Quentin suggests a similar association between the fatal supplement (his sister) and the merely dangerous word: *"My little sister had no. If I could say Mother. Mother."* In his various attempts to defend Caddy's honor, moreover, Quentin recognizes his voice as a weapon that he wields only haltingly and wishfully: *"Quentin has shot . . . Quentin has shot Herbert he shot his voice through the floor of Caddy's room."* Quentin remembers his voice as a threat to intimacy with Caddy; once she asked him to pronounce Dalton Ames's name and to feel her pulse quicken. The episode summarizes Quentin's horror at the intrusion of the voice. Even as his voice arouses, penetrates, fills, possesses, and excites Caddy, it merely travesties their intimacy, for it is all the while proclaiming another. Every spoken word speaks for another—destroying and creating presence, invading immediacy.

The full maturation of his voice, as might have grown out of the trails of narrative in *Absalom* during the previous September, might have freed Quentin to articulate his responses to change and loss through language. He glimpses such an opportunity in his conflict with his father. To put Mr. Compson into words would be to invent him, to gain the authority of authorship over him, to reverse progenitor and son: *"Say it to Father will you I will am my fathers Progenitive I invented him created him Say it to him it will not be for he will say I was not and then you and I since philoprogenitive."* Analogously, a fantastic memory from childhood spells out Quentin's sense of powerlessness before his parents:

> When I was little there was a picture in one of our books, a dark place into which a single weak ray of light came slanting upon two faces lifted out of the shadow. . . . It was torn out, jagged out. I was glad. I'd have to turn back to it until the dungeon was Mother herself she and Father upward into weak light holding hands and us lost somewhere below even them without even a ray of light.

The image of mother as dungeon of course suggests the regressive pull of Quentin's vision, since he yearns for the bliss of the womb, the most secure intimacy of mother, brother, and sister. But that the two faces of Caddy and Quentin are imprisoned in the darkened page of a book suggests that they are embryonically enclosed in the parents' book, incapable of speaking their deliverance. Quentin readily admits to his father that his confession of incest has been a feeble lie, for example, and consequently abandons the potential flight to a more elaborate fiction. In fact, the best measure of Quentin's willed silence occurs in the closing passages of his monologue. The conversation between father and son deliberately flouts the manner of an authentic exchange. It is cast in a stream-of-consciousness style that does not encourage the reader to distinguish the voices through the setting, description, tone, gesture. Instead, the two voices are both versions of Quentin's own. No memory but an invention, as Faulkner confirmed later,

Quentin's thought does not fully create his father's voice at all. Unlike the rich detail of Sutpen's performance in *Absalom* that Quentin and Shreve concoct, this alien voice has nothing but a few well-worn ideas to call its own. Quentin seeks to silence his father's voice by internalizing it, and consequently what masquerades as a debate is actually a double-voiced soliloquy, the twin explanation of suicide as both surrender and defiance.

Quentin "explains" his suicide to himself through an internal colloquy because he recognizes that any single gesture may express contradictory sentiments and arouse rival interpretations. (Compare the mysteries spun by Sutpen's unadorned gestures in *Absalom*.) The actual plunge into the Charles, although it is never recounted, might figure self-punishment, narcissistic reunion, exhausted frustration, and so on, as critics have suggested. But I am interested in what the imminence of suicide does to Quentin's memory before he dies. Faulkner's interest in Quentin's death does not involve the symbolism of the act or its direct consequences, but rather what is created by its looming. Sartre supposed that Quentin was like a man looking backward from a moving automobile; the past spread fully behind him, Quentin ignores the future. Extending this idea, Peter Swiggart suggested that Quentin's suicide exerts a retrospective pressure on his experience of the present and his memory of the past which is able to impose a kind of obsessional order (*The Art of Faulkner's Novels*). This seems the right approach to Quentin's suicide, since it is clearly a creative (though surely desperate) gesture. If Quentin wants to erect an "apotheosis in which a temporary state of mind will become symmetrical above the flesh and aware both of itself and of the flesh it will not quite discard you will not even be dead," if he seeks "to isolate [Caddy] out of the loud world" into a "hell" of his own making, he must envision his escape from time as the achievement *of* his life—and not some presumed ghosthood *after* it. The supernaturally eternal is irrelevant to Quentin; he aspires to a temporary state of mind that tricks itself into half believing its liberation from time. Quentin experiences such a state precisely during his suspended last moment, the moment during which he "thinks" his monologue. Such a moment encloses a region populated with memories of childhood, with incidents from his last day which compose an uncanny palimpsest of the past, with many varieties of the lie that Caddy had (had not) been taken with Quentin.

The artifice of imminent death is Quentin's necessary fiction. Imminent death is the supreme negation of time. Death arrests decay and loss: if grief for Caddy is only a "temporary" state of mind, as Mr. Compson avers, then Quentin wants to save at least that from time's dispossession. To think the annihilation of the future is to leave one's memories intact; it dreams an apotheosis of the temporary. It cheats the certainty that "someday it will no longer hurt you like this." Death gives peace to eyes exhausted by seeing the past through the present, by struggling to coerce the absent one to reappear in the flow of time:

> I could not see the bottom, but I could see a long way into the motion of the water before the eye gave out, and then I saw a shadow hanging like a fat arrow stemming into the current.

Death contemplates the ending, completion; it resolves Quentin's fear of having to remember the past endlessly in order to preserve Caddy. "Finished. If things just finished themselves"; "Again. Sadder than was. Again. Saddest of all. Again." Death by suicide kills time and death themselves: Quentin's gesture appropriates to himself the power of time to take away life.

If Sartre had been right about the power of the unchangeable past to invade the present and occupy it wholly, Quentin's desperation would be difficult to explain. It is because "was" does *not* exist that there is grief. For all his furious devotion, Quentin still senses that his memory is incapable of reappropriating the lost Caddy. Critics have pointed to Quentin's "recovery" of whole episodes from his childhood as testimony to his obsessive power of recall. And we have begun to understand how the events of his last day subtly replicate features of his loss of Caddy, as if every present moment is a repetition of the original dispossession. But we may also discover that Quentin's memory necessarily disfigures, corrects, and structures the past so as to satisfy a fundamental ambivalence: he yearns to recover the plenitude, unity, and innocence of Caddy at the same time that he confronts the fact that to remember Caddy is to insist on her absence or death. Like Benjy, he can remember Caddy only as the presence that has already begun to vanish. Similarly, the events of the last day, although they coincide with the past remarkably, nevertheless retain their stubborn difference. Incidents play in counterpoint across the years, but Quentin's imagination shapes the contingent present into a supplement of the past that is lost.

As Quentin spends his last afternoon trying to return a lost little girl to her family, his memory opens access to the moments of his own childhood that have witnessed the disappearance of a sister. Quentin's anxiety has been to evade sexual maturation because it constitutes initiation into a fallen world of sexual difference, procreation, and death, the fruits of time. When Caddy once discovers him in the barn with Natalie, he insists on their innocence: *"You know what I was doing? . . . I was hugging her that's what I was doing."* Quentin evokes this moment precisely because it both creates the appearance of his own defection to adulthood and also deliberately denies it. It tests his power to call sexual passion mere brotherly affection and to convert an opportunity to lose his virginity into an occasion to defend it. The second phase of this incident elaborates the duplicity of Quentin's memory, for he remembers chastizing Caddy for her failure to care as much for his virginity as he does for hers. When she turns back to say, *"I don't give a damn what you were doing,"* he protests paradoxically by burlesquing an act of intercourse with her:

> She hit my hands away I smeared mud on her with the other
> hand I couldn't feel the wet smacking of her hand I wiped mud
> from my legs smeared it on her wet hard turning body.

The performance expresses both Quentin's attempt to preserve Caddy's virginity and his recognition that he can remember her only as already contaminated by the filth of sex. Moreover, it casts him as both defender and despoiler; his memory imagines a scene that satisfies the lie of incest. These divergent qualities are important because they confirm that Caddy may never be reappropriated as absolute innocence. The persistence of these memories derives from the beginning of difference; memory supplements as it recalls a past that is already dead.

A second arrangement of these tensions appears when Quentin recollects threatening Caddy with a penknife. As many readers have noticed, this scene illuminates Quentin's neurotic identification of sex and death and prefigures the consummation of impotence in suicide. But it also responds to Quentin's need to fuse the nostalgia for innocent prepossession to the knowledge of Caddy's disappearance. The moment begins by associating sexual exposure and death ("do you remember the day damuddy died when you sat down in the water in your drawers"). And, of course, the knife that murders is the phallus that penetrates. As the sequence of events presses toward climax, Quentin's impotence overrules:

> what is it what are you doing
> her muscles gathered I sat up
> its my knife I dropped it
> she sat up
> what time is it
> I dont know

The moment that Quentin recreates interrupts deathly intercourse before it can reenact Caddy's slaughter, but the long scene continues until Quentin eventually remembers passing his sister on to Dalton Ames, who does kill her (*"did you love them Caddy did you love them When they touched me I died"*). Almost-intercourse is exactly what Quentin might hope to imagine to himself endlessly. An eternal suspension at the instant between virginity and penetration, between childhood and adulthood, when no one asks what time it is, would enable Quentin never to lose Caddy because he had never possessed her. The incompletion, paradoxical tension, and displacement (substituting himself tentatively for the actual lover who kills Caddy) allow Quentin to play out his desire to possess Caddy while evading the murder by phallus. In these moments he possesses Caddy fully in her virginity; he enjoys an innocent incest.

Once Quentin has committed his memory to filling the vacuum of Caddy's loss, the supplemental properties of all substitution obstruct his naive efforts to simply reappropriate her. His memory persistently threatens to transform the sense of Caddy's absence into the story of her loss. One may see the discursive qualities of Quentin's vision in the fictive image patterns of his section: the gulls of timelessness, the clocks of time-bound-edness, for example. When he remembers his vain effort to banish Dalton Ames, moreover, he conjures a scene worthy of any Western melodrama. (Can we be sure Quentin hasn't even made up this outlaw suitor's name?) He finds Ames rolling a cigarette with one hand, demonstrating his sharp-shooting, and smiling at Quentin's ultimatum to get out of town by sun-down. Quentin locates their confrontation on a bridge; the two struggle over the branch about the body of Caddy. Ames picks bark chips from the bridge and shoots them as they flick into the water below, a taut image of the potency of his phallicism and the abandonment of Caddy (who smells like trees) to the flux. Quentin fails to hold his position on the bridge and faints like a girl after feebly voicing his objection to Ames's suit. The scene dramatizes Quentin's inability to bestride the waters of sex and time, and dooms him to flight. Satisfied with such symbolically charged vignettes, however, Quentin silences his voice just before it breaks into story.

The past that Quentin's memory represents is not the original, natural reality; it is the half-remembered, half-invented domain of a necessarily transfigured childhood. That transfiguration extends into Quentin's un-canny reliving of the past during his last day. Quentin's memory has been so magnetized by Caddy's loss that when he looks back from his last moment on the events of the preceding afternoon they seem to reenact her disappearance. His effort to restore the "little sister" to her home and his vain assault on the crowing Gerald Bland surely figure Quentin's childhood attempts to reclaim Caddy and to fight off Dalton Ameses and Herbert

Heads. The narrative segments of the afternoon of June 2 occasion "memories" of corresponding events in the sequence of Caddy's loss; the passages alternate, creating a sense of repetition. But if the episodes of the past fail to re-present the natural, innocent Caddy herself, as I have argued, the incidents of the afternoon also inevitably misshape the past. Quentin corrects the past as he relives it.

That Quentin calls the Italian child "little sister" leaves us no doubt about his association, but earlier in his monologue he has wondered about the "good Saint Francis that said Little Sister Death, that never had a sister." The child embodies not the lost innocent sister but her ghost. Quentin sees her as unknowingly contaminated by sexuality: when she accepts coins from Quentin, her "fingers [close] about them, damp and hot, like worms," an image that reflects Quentin's horror of the phallic and his usual attribution of masculine power to Caddy. After the shoplady's warning that the girl will "hide [the loaf] under her dress and a body'd never know it," the child accompanies him through the rain with the tip of the loaf peering out of its wrapper ("the nose of the loaf naked"). Quentin's fumbling impotence in the rain with his penknife corresponds to his futile attempt to protect the loaf; as he looks at "the half-naked loaf clutched to her breast," he begins to "wipe the loaf, but the crust began to come off, so I stopped." Quentin's gesture seems to resign custody of the phallus to the little girl and to accept its erosion by water. Perhaps the act figures the "mutilation" and "castration" that Caddy's loss means to Quentin. Quentin's dealings with this reincarnation of Caddy suggest that she is a substitute whose difference from the original prompts him to confirm rather than overcome the deadness of the past.

Shortly after this incident, Quentin experiences another moment that reveals the differences between past and present. He and "sister" surprise several boys swimming naked. As the two approach the water, Quentin chillingly predicts his suicide: " 'Hear them in swimming, sister? I wouldn't mind doing that myself.' If I had time. When I had time. I could hear my watch." To join Caddy, naked in the waters of death; to rejoin her in the mud of the river, in the branch of childhood; to master time finally and flee the ticking are suicidal fantasies. But Quentin recoils for the moment, as if yearning for a revision of the past that would pardon them from the original fall. The boys are embarrassed by their nakedness and shout:

> "Take that girl away! What did you want to bring a girl here for? Go on away!"
> "She wont hurt you. We just want to watch you for a while."

If "sister" only watches the naked adolescents, she and Quentin can enact a past that never was. If only Caddy had never disrobed to enter the branch, the voices "o'er Eden" might still call to each other. When the boys threaten to "get out and throw them in," Quentin and little sister leave: " 'That's not for us, is it.' "

The entire climactic scene of little sister's shadowing Quentin resounds with echoes of his loss of Caddy. The little girl's refusal to leave her new love drives Quentin to long for parental responsibility ("if you could just slice the walls away all of a sudden Madam, your daughter, if you please. No. Madam, for God's sake, your daughter"; and "Your papa's going to be worried about you"). After the child's brother finally spies the "kidnapper" and his victim, he launches a pursuit, followed by two of the naked swimmers. "You steela my seester" elicits Quentin's hysterical laughter at the ironic repetition. Like Ames, Quentin makes off with a sister; but Julio, his two naked companions, and an older officer promptly seek her recovery. That quartet stands in mute antithesis to the trio of impotent brothers and the helpless father who witness Caddy's disappearance. The episodes of Quentin's last day are compelled by the focus of his memory to resemble the scenes of Caddy's loss; and yet they never become transparent replications of the past, nor do they even allow an untroubled reemergence of Caddy in memory. Instead, Quentin's monologue presents a Caddy who can be only a supplement to that illusory, originary presence. Memory, speech, and desire may be activated only by a sense of loss that can never know original possession; and their pleasures depend on the continued sense of difference, spacing, and death. These are the conditions for articulation.

Precarious Coherence: Objects through Time

Gail L. Mortimer

> *As though the clotting which is you had dissolved into the myriad original motion.*
>
> As I Lay Dying

When we look closely at Faulkner's descriptions of objects and activities that exist through the course of time, we discover that his perceptual style continues to rely heavily on the imagistic visualization of his concern with transience. Faulkner is never able to leave behind his awareness that the life around him is pervaded by change, and his descriptions visually suggest this preoccupation by focusing on disintegration taking place at objects' surfaces and by avoiding direct descriptions of motion in favor of oblique approaches, such as creating "frozen moments" or "tableaux." As he depicts motion and the existence of objects in time, his prose expresses a continuing awareness of time's ravages.

As various critics have noted, Faulkner's prose reveals a number of affinities with the thoughts of Henri Bergson on the nature of reality and our perception of it. Bergson held that whether we believe the fundamental component of life to be mind or matter, our intuitive understanding forces us to acknowledge that life is characterized by its quality of continuous change, or "becoming." He calls this perpetual becoming "flux"; it involves life's ongoing emergence into potentials that are never fully realized, since that would be the end of change and, hence, death. Flux is the essential feature both of physical substances (or objects) and of mental processes.

From *Faulkner's Rhetoric of Loss: A Study in Perception and Meaning.* © 1983 by the University of Texas Press.

One cannot be the same person on two separate occasions, for example, because we cannot live the same moment twice. Our existence through time involves a perpetual accumulation of experiences, each of which alters the sum of our previous experiences. It is evident, in this view, that we can never return to any moment in the past, for intervening moments have irrevocably altered us.

This accretion of events—the omnipresence of the past in the evolving present—gives to our experience of time a quality that Bergson calls "durée" or "duration." Although it is not possible to verify the source for Faulkner's use of the term, we cannot help but think of his famous synopsis of the lives of such figures as Dilsey, found in his 1945 Appendix to *The Sound and the Fury:* "They endured." For Faulkner, endurance involves precisely an awareness of the multifariousness of accumulating experience and of the fullness of life. There are significant differences between this type of existence, which connotes serenity and an acceptance of things as they are, and the simple tenacity evinced by those Faulknerian characters who live in the past. Their lives are effectively over, as Faulkner reminds us repeatedly in imagery of deadness and stagnation. We have seen this already in the figures of Emily Grierson, Joanna Burden, and Gail Hightower, whose antipathy to life is vividly suggested in false pregnancies and similar grotesqueries. To accept the present moment with its myriad implications is to grow with it and change because of it. The rigidity of not being able to do so is the source of much anguish for Faulkner's time-entrapped characters.

In spite of our intuition's recognition of the fluidity of experience, Bergson argued, our rational faculty is able to contemplate the realities presented to it only by assuming a stability that contradicts our subjective experience of flux and duration. Immanuel Kant had recognized this characteristic of the rational mind when he asserted that "space" and "time" are forms of perception which organize a priori the experience of all phenomena. We are incapable of thinking of anything without spatializing it—which intrinsically assumes a degree of finitude and stability—or temporalizing it in a manner that assumes linearity and succession and, again, finitude. As Bergson describes it:

> Preoccupied before everything with the necessities of action, the intellect, like the senses, is limited to taking, at intervals, views that are instantaneous and by that very fact immobile of the becoming of matter. . . . Of becoming we perceive only states, of duration only instants, and even when we speak of duration and of becoming, it is of another thing that we are thinking.

Such is the most striking of the two illusions we wish to examine.
It consists in supposing that we can think the unstable by means
of the stable, the moving by means of the immobile.

(Creative Evolution)

This is the paradox that underlies Faulkner's apparently self-contradictory manner of depicting motion and change. On the one hand, he continually tries to come to terms with and describe the flux of experience, including its subjective urgency, its elusiveness, and its ephemerality. On the other, while he is doing so, his prose expresses a need to control described objects, especially affectively potent ones, by spatializing them: seeing them in strongly visual terms, splitting them apart, focusing on the boundaries that separate and define them as distinct from one another, and so on. The rhythm of flowing and control that I explicate . . . is a rhythm created by his relative stressing of (1) the flux of experience as it tends to flow with its own momentum and (2) the illusion of stability implicit in asserting the finitude or boundedness of objects in this same reality.

On occasions when Faulkner and Bergson attempt to describe the subjective experience of continuity through time and change, they have chosen remarkably similar imagery. Describing the passage of time, Faulkner frequently imagines roads, tunnels, and corridors, which appear to close behind us and open at our approach, as time does. In a similar way, Bergson has chosen to discuss his own "mental state, as it advances on the road of time . . . continually swelling with the duration which it accumulates." Each of them has chosen a finite, visual representation to suggest the distinction between the *apparent* linearity and succession of time and the subjectively *experienced* fullness of the moments in which we exist.

One of Faulkner's omnipresent images is that of a moving object, often explicitly likened to a bead, on a wire or string. As we have seen, in the first chapter of *Light in August,* Lena Grove perceives a wagon in such terms as it moves through time and space, both as it approaches her on the road and as she later rides on it. The wagon is alternately described as a "shabby bead" and as a "spool" onto which the "mild red string of road" is being rewound. Compare this with Bergson as he writes about the illusory nature of states of being, in this instance, the "mental states" of the "ego": "Instead of a flux of fleeting shades merging into each other, [our reason] perceives distinct and, so to speak, *solid* colors, set side by side like the beads of a necklace; it must perforce then suppose a thread, also itself solid, to hold the beads together." Bergson compares our perception of the relationship between states of mind and the ego—and implicitly between any "states" of being and the concept which subsumes them—with that of beads on a thread. He tells us that the distinct entities that reason sees when it focuses on outer reality, as well as the continuity that we posit as we try to comprehend that reality, are illusory. Such *merely apparent* relationships are belied by the radical flux of experience. Faulkner, of course, has used the same imagery to describe the same circumstance—a character's perception of apparent continuity as she waits through time for the arrival and observes the progress of a wagon.

Faulkner habitually uses such images as spools, beads, and tunnels when he tries to assert the stability or sameness of people or objects that move through time and space. This technique is especially evident in Quentin's monologue in *The Sound and the Fury*. As we shall see later in this chapter, Quentin's obsessive need to control his perceptions, because it gives him the illusion of controlling reality, results in a variety of idiosyncratic imaginings, among them his recurrent perception of such figures as birds being suspended between the branches of trees (or the sails of ships) on wires or being dragged by wires through space. This narrative technique and similar ones—in which notably visual images anchor and spatialize (even geometrize) what Faulkner is describing—help Faulkner to bypass the direct description of such phenomena as motion or change by "freezing" the event being described (the flight of birds) into a seemingly stable visual configuration in which everything is "connected" to everything else. An effect of such metaphorical language—intrinsically indirect—is that his descriptions seem to retain the elusiveness of experience. By displacing motion and change themselves onto metaphors, Faulkner acts out the inherent resistance of experience to direct description. He avoids "killing" what he describes by doing so obliquely.

To describe an object existing through time, Faulkner is forced to deal with the differences that characterize an object from one moment to another. He is conscious both of the transience and intangibility of mere qualities and of the inexpressibility of essences, those fundamental characteristics that allow each of us to remain somehow recognizable as ourselves. . . . Faulkner habitually controls objects in proximity to one another, that is to say, how he confronts the problem of describing differences between objects coexisting in space. The differences within a single object from one moment to the next are the temporal equivalent of that descriptive problem. In both instances, Faulkner focuses his energies on a consideration of the surfaces or edges of things. Just as he emphasized boundaries to assert one object's distinctness from other objects, he also uses them in ways that allow an inference of change or flux within a single object. In other words, he uses boundaries paradoxically, both to emphasize an object's autonomy and separateness and to reveal its fluidity and the precariousness of its identity. This should remind us of the developmental task I outlined [elsewhere]: the need to establish a sense of self separate from other objects in the world and yet be able to interact meaningfully with that world (go beyond one's felt boundaries) without feeling that one's identity is being lost, the need to be both separate from and connected to others.

Objects in Faulkner's fictive world tend to display at their surfaces an aura, a penumbra, an emanation—where they are not quite fully themselves but are evolving into something different that they have not quite yet become. Like the rays of the sun in *The Sound and the Fury,* they begin to assume new identities: "Sunlight slanted into it, sparse and eager. Yellow butterflies flickered along the shade like flecks of sun"; "Sunlight . . . glinting along the pole like yellow ants"; "pencils of sun slanted in the trees"; "Little flecks of sunlight brushing across my face like yellow leaves"; "There was another yellow butterfly, like one of the sunflecks had come loose." . . .

The rhetoric of Quentin Compson's monologue in *The Sound and the Fury* reveals the modes of perception of one explicitly preoccupied with the passage of time. Again, we have before us a slightly exaggerated instance of language reflecting a constant awareness of change and loss—by virtue of the obsessions that dominate everything Quentin does—but we see a perceptual style that, nevertheless, illuminates our understanding of more typical ways of looking at the world characteristic of even the omniscient narrators in Faulkner's stories. As Quentin experiences his world flowing out of control, his perceptions increasingly involve the spatializing of all of his sensations and thoughts in a manifest attempt to manage reality through the illusion of control that is innate to vision. Quentin, through Faulkner, virtually geometrizes the objects he encounters to control their relationships to one another and himself, and his story abounds with horizontal and vertical lines, oblique lines, bridges and lanes, frames (mirrors, doorways, watch faces), enclosed spaces or spaces that feel like vacuums, and rhythmically regular segments of both time and space. The world itself undermines his efforts to keep things stable as it fragments, flows, and changes through time despite Quentin's vigilance. From the first words onward, Quentin's monologue expresses his struggle with time as he searches for timeless (that is, purely spatial, stable) modes of perception. Time is transformed into a place to be—"then I was in time again, hearing the watch"—but it is also his enemy because it is where change irrevocably occurs.

Quentin's radical spatializing is an attempt to reverse the effects of time, specifically to undo the changes that have occurred in Caddy as her emerging sexuality has left him behind by totally changing their relationship. Quentin wants to recapture their reliance on one another and their intimacy by controlling and turning back time. As we shall see, he accomplishes this symbolically in his death.

Among the perceptions that dominate the monologue are those of Quentin's nihilistic father, Jason, which Quentin struggles unsuccessfully to deny. In Jason Compson's view, man is a pathetic combination of molecules and experiences doomed to fade quickly into anonymity and meaninglessness. Quentin tries to establish "importance" in his universe—a semblance of immortality, something that does not fade with time—but he is undermined by his father's vision of things: "Father was teaching us that all men are just accumulations dolls stuffed with sawdust swept up from the trash heaps where all previous dolls had been thrown away the sawdust flowing from what wound in what side that not for me died not"; "Man the sum of his climatic [sic] experiences Father said. Man the sum of what have you. A problem in impure properties carried tediously to an unvarying nil: stalemate of dust and desire." Instead of flesh and blood, inanimate entities coalesce to form mankind. There is no hope of achieving identity or importance in such a world, and we recognize in Quentin's efforts to reify such notions as honor, virginity, and his imagined incest with Caddy—all of which, because they are insubstantial, cannot fade—attempts to defy the dissolution that besets everything around him. Jason recognizes the illusoriness of such an imaginative control of one's perceptions: "you wanted to sublimate a piece of natural human folly into a horror and then exorcise it"; "you are not thinking of finitude you are contemplating an apotheosis in which a temporary state of mind will become symmetrical above the flesh and aware both of itself and of the flesh it will not quite discard . . . you cannot bear to think that someday it will no longer hurt you like this."

The dissolution of Quentin's world is also suggested in the precariousness of his sense of self, especially evident in his relationship with his own shadow, that penumbral part of himself that he seems to regard as perversely having an existence of its own. A walk becomes an occasion to trick his shadow into merging with water or other shadows, to trample it into the pavement and the dust, and to walk on its belly. As a dimension of his own surface, Quentin's shadow is important because it shows us his preoccupation with control, literally with self-control. Perhaps his shadow, with its darkness and fluidity, represents the dark, soft, feminine aspect of

Quentin and, as such, threatens him with a loss of his sense of himself; this meaning would certainly be consistent with our understanding of the similar dilemma in Joe Christmas. The shadow's easy merging with ground, water, trees, and other shadows through its softness and malleability suggests its affinities with the feminine. Quentin is only able to react to its flowing by asserting rigidity and control, by successfully "tricking" it. It is clear, though, that his shadow, as part of his surface, evades definition and management. It preserves its essential fluidity and, in doing so, serves as an appropriate focus for Quentin's absorption with the existence and potential annihilation of his own identity. His death plunges him into fusion with his shadow: "Niggers say a drowned man's shadow was watching for him in the water all the time."

Given Quentin's preoccupations in this monologue, it is not surprising that the descriptive passages here constantly play with boundaries and their various degrees of tangibility. Descriptions reminding us of figure-ground reversal are everywhere, as in the dozens of references to patches of sunlight and shadows. The two are, obviously, different aspects of the same phenomenon, an interaction of light and darkness. Faulkner even uses the image of a stencil to bring us both possibilities at once in an explicit figure-ground image: "The shadows on the road were as still as if they had been put there with a stencil, with slanting pencils of sunlight."

On other occasions Faulkner creates the effect of blurred experience by using synesthetic devices, either combining sound, smell, and sight or time and space or using one to describe the other. Thus, he speaks of *"the twilight-coloured smell of honeysuckle"* and of Gerald Bland, pulling his oars "in lonely state across the noon, rowing himself right out of noon, up the long bright air like an apotheosis, mounting into a drowsing infinity." He also describes the sound of a bell in terms of the space and silence that are its ambience: "When you opened the door a bell tinkled, but just once, high and clear and small in the neat obscurity above the door, as though it were gauged and tempered to make that single clear small sound so as not to wear the bell out nor to require the expenditure of too much silence in restoring it." And again, "I ran down the hill in that vacuum of crickets . . . the air seemed to drizzle with honeysuckle and with the rasping of crickets a substance you could feel on the flesh." The effect he achieves by crossing these conceptual boundaries is the heightened intensity of the perception itself and a more convincing sense of experience, of reality. Each perception seems to be suspended among the possibilities implied by the multiple modes of perception that interact to reveal it, rather than being confined by a neat and finite correlation between the sense and the object perceived. In passages of this type we are encouraged as readers to accept the interchangeability of color, sound, smell, touch, and concept as evidence of the potency of experiences that are charged with meaning for his characters. This synesthetic description is consistent, too, with our earlier recognition that sound and smell are more potent indicators of reality for Faulkner's characters than sight. The interiority of sound and smell signifies subjectively that borders have been crossed (our own), just as synesthesia intensifies perceptions by providing that same illusion.

In the monologue preceding Quentin's, that of his retarded brother Benjy, a group of objects of various shapes, smells, and colors (especially red) comfort Benjy as substitutes for his sister Caddy, whom Faulkner is careful to tell us Benjy "could not remember . . . but only the loss of her." Benjy loves three things: his sister, the pasture sold to pay for her wedding and send Quentin to Harvard, and firelight. But the associations of these things are virtually interchangeable. Firelight is "the same bright shape as going to sleep," and Caddy smells "like when she says we were asleep." Her "hair was like fire, and little points of fire were in her eyes . . . and Caddy held me." Caddy often smells "like trees," "like leaves," and "like trees in the rain." Benjy's comforting bright shapes include the red cushion (like fire, warm, smells of Caddy), Caddy's slipper (warm, smells of Caddy), and the pasture with its trees, leaves, and grass. These are the reassuring smells, connected to his dim remembrance of the warmth she represented to him. Moreover, Benjy experiences all intense realities in terms of smell: death (Damuddy's), sickness (Mother's), the cold, the perfume symbolizing Caddy's unfamiliar sexuality, and the change as Caddy gets married. The narrative associations reflect his intense, if primitive, perceptions as he intuits the crucial truths about changes in his family.

Benjy is quite different from the cerebral, tormented Quentin, yet his experiences prepare us for a corresponding group of associations that trigger Quentin's memories of his sister, associations as complex with implications as Benjy's are straightforward. Quentin's thoughts about Caddy are fraught with many of the associations to the female that we encountered in *Light in August*. She and women in general are linked with death ("the good Saint Francis that said Little Sister Death, that never had a sister"), with evil ("*they have an affinity for evil*"), with the potent smell of honeysuckle, which symbolizes sexuality as a pervasive and threatening presence, with the color red (blood, passion, roses, "*Red print of my hand coming up through her face*"), and with the earth, the pasture, and water (Caddy up in a tree with muddy drawers and lying in the river). The entire episode in which Quentin walks near the river in Boston and tries to rid himself of the little Italian girl, whom he always addresses as "sister," is interspersed with his memories of times when he and Caddy were in or near the river near their home. These are sexually powerful occasions when Quentin tries to make Caddy explain her relationships with men and her pregnancy and when they nearly complete a mutual suicide (itself described in distinctly sexual terms).

The appeal of water, in fact, permeates Quentin's monologue. It is often in the background or in his thoughts. "I could smell the curves of the river beyond the dusk"; "I can be dead in Harvard Caddy said in the caverns and the grottoes of the sea tumbling peacefully to the wavering tides." After his fight with Dalton Ames over Caddy, Quentin "couldnt hear anything but the water." There is reason to believe that the river and Caddy are closely associated in Quentin's mind, that indeed the river may stand for her in an important way. Earlier Faulkner stories reveal experiments with these psychic associations. In "The Kid Learns" Faulkner substituted for a death scene his young hoodlum protagonist's meeting of a girl with "eyes the color of sleep" who introduced herself as "Little Sister Death." In an allegory Faulkner wrote for his friend Helen Baird, a wounded knight frees himself from his companions Hunger and Pain by joining a maiden called "Little Sister Death" and then drowning himself in a river. Other early stories reveal similar configurations: sisters and brothers, confusions of rivers with sleep or death, and an innocent sleeping together of brothers and sisters that anticipates Faulkner's later, complex incestuous relationships in such works as The Sound and the Fury and Absalom, Absalom!

William Niederland has written an essay entitled "The Symbolic River-Sister Equation in Poetry and Folklore," which suggests that this symbol derives from maternal images (water as the source of life) and birth fantasies. Both reflect the universal symbolism of water as "embracing life, birth, love, guilt, and death." Niederland relates several mythical tales in which brothers and sisters, apparently as punishment for unconscious incestuous desires, are turned into rivers or into animals by drinking from rivers or (as in The Mill on the Floss) drown together or in which (as in Byron's Childe Harold's Pilgrimage) rivers carry a seductive appeal that only thinly disguises feelings for one's sister. He cites clinical material from several analysts affirming that such associations are common in the fantasies and dreams of patients.

Whether or not Faulkner has drawn from some mythic or psychic symbolic equation, he has in Quentin's case, as critic André Bleikasten has noted, made explicit connections between Caddy and rivers. After he fights with Dalton Ames on a bridge over a river (over Caddy, as it were), Quentin is haunted by memories of the river at home, is fascinated with the river in Boston, and finally drowns himself there. It is both the end of his suffering and the culmination of his desire. His death acts out a fusion with Caddy: his desire for union with her and the annihilation of the personal distinctions that have made them separate people: "I will look down and see my murmuring bones and the deep water like wind, like a roof of wind, and after a long time they cannot distinguish even bones upon the lonely and inviolate sand." Psychologically, Quentin's suicide simultaneously fulfills his incestuous longing and allows him to punish himself for it. His love of death and his love for Caddy are nearly equated in this passage that emphasizes the tension he feels between maintaining a necessary distance (keeping the boundaries clear) and completely immersing himself into the other that he longs for: Quentin, "who loved death above all, who loved only death, loved and lived in a deliberate and almost perverted anticipation of death as a lover loves and deliberately refrains from the waiting willing friendly tender incredible body of his beloved, until he can no longer bear not the refraining but the restraint and so flings, hurls himself, relinquishing, drowning." Bleikasten shares my belief that "in Faulkner's fiction the perils of sex are often described in terms of engulfment, and drowning is a recurrent metaphor for the vertigo of lust." Quentin's is an immersion into the Conradian "destructive element."

Quentin's death, moreover, and his trip through the secret waters to "the caverns and the grottoes of the sea" is reminiscent of another womb-like place that appeals to him: "When I was little there was a picture in one of our books, a dark place into which a single weak ray of light came slanting upon two faces lifted out of the shadow. . . . It was torn out, jagged out. I was glad. I'd have to turn back to it until the dungeon was Mother herself she and Father upward into weak light holding hands and us lost somewhere below even them without even a ray of light. Then the honeysuckle got into it." Quentin sees himself and Caddy together in a dark place apart from their parents, not yet born, just as elsewhere he envisions himself and Caddy in hell, encircled by flame but isolated and together. The honeysuckle (signaling the passage of time and the coming of sexuality) interrupts this fantasy, but Quentin's manner of dying has the effect of reversing time and sends him back to the state of uncreation represented when he and Caddy were in the dungeon of their mother. This remarkable visual image allows Quentin to be both undefined (= unborn = fused with Caddy = beyond the power of time to change them) and safely within a boundary (womb, dungeon, grotto, cavern, circle in Hell) that excludes the rest of the world. Then "it would be as though it had never been." "A quarter hour yet. And then I'll not be. The peacefullest words. Peacefullest words. *Non fui. Sum. Fui. Nom sum.*"

In a passage near the end of Quentin's monologue, his multiple associations to Caddy appear, recur, and circle back on one another, creating an intensity that expresses Quentin's growing obsession with his sister and the centripetal movement toward fusion even of his perceptions as they foreshadow the manner of his death:

> I could see the twilight again, that quality of light as if time really had stopped for a while . . . and the road going on under the twilight, into twilight and the sense of water peaceful and swift beyond. . . . Honeysuckle was the saddest odour of all, I think. I remember lots of them. Wistaria was one. . . .
>
> I could feel water beyond the twilight, smell. When it bloomed in the spring and it rained the smell was everywhere you didnt notice it so much at other times but when it rained the smell began to come into the house at twilight either it would rain more at twilight or there was something in the light itself but it always smelled strongest then until I would lie in bed thinking when will it stop when will it stop. The draft in the door smelled of water, a damp steady breath. Sometimes I could put myself to sleep saying that over and over until after the honeysuckle got all mixed up in it the whole thing came to symbolise night and unrest I seemed to be lying neither asleep nor awake looking down a long corridor of grey halflight where all stable things had become shadowy paradoxical all I had done shadows all I had felt suffered taking visible form antic and perverse mocking without relevance inherent themselves with the denial of the significance they should have affirmed.

Twilight, which dominates this passage, is a recurring and important symbol in Faulkner's stories. Compressed into this one concept are many of the implications of his thoughts about transience and the nature of the lived moment. It suggests exactly the precarious coherence that characterizes the universe Quentin perceives, and *Twilight* was, in fact, the original title of Faulkner's *The Sound and the Fury*.

Especially insofar as it presents a descriptive problem, twilight expresses the diffusion of qualities and imperfect clarity that are characteristic of the surfaces of objects in Faulkner's fictive world. The moment of twilight is at once intense and indeterminate. Visually, it is a fusion of light and dark, of white and black. Its essential feature *is* the flowing that carries it so quickly away, and the concept by which we think of the phenomenon "twilight" is one of those immobile entities that Bergson tells us typify the illusion that we are thinking of becoming itself. Twilight is quintessentially a blurring of sensations and boundaries, just as any subjectively experienced event is. Its fugacity also suggests the fundamental inexpressibility in words of events and personalities. A description of either an event or a person necessarily involves the illusions of unity and finitude that Bergson shows us are belied by experience. The flowing of temporal and spatial phenomena into one another is far closer to the experience of flux.

When we describe twilight, moreover, we can do it only by referring to what precedes and what follows it. In one case we have dusk; in the other, dawn. In this sense it is like any present moment in Faulkner's stories. Its intensity or essence is never described in isolation; Faulkner invariably provides a spatial and temporal ambience that confirms it meaning. In his prose, antecedents, subsequences, and environment become a major focus of narrative energy. Consequently, his descriptions are often more implied than actual as he exercises some of the possibilities of figure-ground techniques. Using synesthesia, oxymora, and neologisms, Faulkner is able to preserve the myriad possibilities inherent in the description of something as a direct description can scarely do as well. The reader infers, connects hints, and fills in gaps to participate in creating the meanings Faulkner evokes. There are crucial absences everywhere in his stories, as we will explore more fully [elsewhere].

In a number of descriptive passages the moment of twilight and the experience of watching it are conjoined, quite appropriately, with an awareness of the sensations of sound and smell (as with Gail Hightower and Quentin Compson). The humming of insects, the murmuring of voices, the smell of honeysuckle (elsewhere, verbena or wisteria), and a fading of the visual scene reinforce the sense of a relaxation of boundaries or distinctions, just as they suggest a concomitant increase in subjective intensity. Vast numbers of characters experience special insights, make decisions, begin and finish journeys, go through crises, are born, and die at twilight (both dawn and dusk) in Faulkner's world. "It seemed to him that he could see the yellow day opening peacefully on before him, like a corridor, an arras, into a still chiaroscuro without urgency."

The titles of Faulkner's works are also revealing. In much of his major fiction, his titles reflect an awareness of the evanescence of moments and experiences: the hum of mosquitoes, the pervasiveness of dust, haunting smells, the quality of a moment, the quintessential and the intangible. The quality of light is an important focus: *Dark House* was the working title of both *Light in August* and *Absalom, Absalom!* evoking that dark, womblike place from within which we have seen Hightower look out at twilight and Quentin at weak maternal light. His titles often reflect times ("Dry September," "Delta Autumn," "That Evening Sun," *Light in August*) because moments in time carry with them an elusiveness that is central to his vision.

Twilight involves yet another meaning relevant to Faulkner's perceptual style. It involves "a period of decline," the passing of something into a lesser state, ultimately toward death or absence. In a larger sense, of course, Faulkner sees the Southern experience itself as an attempt to cope with the degeneration of its culture following the Civil War, with the loss of what it was before 1861. But throughout his fiction, as we have begun to see, it is the deterioration, fading away, death, and absence of important things that preoccupies Faulkner, his narrators, and his characters.

The Myth of *The Sound and the Fury*

Eric J. Sundquist

There is some irony in the fact that Faulkner's deserved public recognition came at a time (the late 1940s and on to his death) when his best work was a decade old and he was writing some of the most disappointing fiction a major novelist could conceivably write. Little that he produced after *Go Down, Moses,* including *Intruder in the Dust,* the novel that guaranteed that recognition, merits sustained attention. The larger irony is that once we begin backtracking to see where he went wrong we must return to the novel often taken to be his masterpiece. With fanfare Faulkner surely would have relished and did his best to facilitate, *The Sound and the Fury* (1929) has become a myth. No one would want to deny its importance, but it is worthwhile considering where, exactly, that importance lies. The novel has been so thoroughly explicated that it should prove more useful to read it with an eye to its place at the starting point of Faulkner's career and in the larger self-imposed design of his fiction, a design one may certainly admire without taking altogether seriously.

The Sound and the Fury is not, of course, the starting point of Faulkner's career. He had already written three novels: *Soldiers' Pay* (1926), a good postwar novel, which unevenly rivals Dos Passos and Hemingway; *Mosquitoes* (1927), a dismal tract on aestheticism; and *Sartoris* (1929), a powerful historical novel improved by editorial revisions of its original, *Flags in the Dust.* Beyond that, he had written two volumes worth of *fin de siècle* poetry and a handful of short stories, some of which were later incorporated into

From *Faulkner: The House Divided.* © 1983 by The Johns Hopkins University Press, Baltimore/London.

novels, or—in the case of *The Sound and the Fury*—blossomed into whole novels, or got added to others and then posed as novels. Without *The Sound and the Fury* and the work that followed, however, few of these earlier efforts would get more than a glance. And there is reason to believe that without Faulkner's work of the next ten years *The Sound and the Fury* would itself seem a literary curiosity, an eccentric masterpiece of experimental methods and "modernist" ideas. This states the worst case, as it were, and proposes the unknowable. But Faulkner's insistent announcements (to choose one of many examples) that the novel was "the most gallant, the most magnificent failure" of all his failed works, and that he therefore loved it most, make inevitable its glamorous position at the dawn of his creation. This is not to say that *The Sound and the Fury* is not a superior novel but simply that it prefigures many problems in Faulkner's later fiction and is far too likely to appear the monumental work against which his other fiction must be judged.

Faulkner vigorously promoted this view (and apparently subscribed to it himself), and any reading of his career in whole or in part will necessarily depend on it. One may, nevertheless, accept the novel as his moment of discovered genius without concluding that it is the key to the treasure of Yoknapatawpha. It would not be apparent until after his death, when two versions of an introduction he wrote and discarded in 1933 were published, what a burden the novel would have to carry. The introduction says more eloquently what Faulkner had always said in public—that the novel was a wonderful failure, a story so great that it could not be put into words, and had produced in him an ecstasy he had never been able to recapture; but the appendix exposes something more unsettling—that the muse of Yoknapatawpha was in decline, that her author was struggling to extend his great design out of any odds and ends he could dream up. The appendix adds, in the ponderous, often absurd prose that is characteristic of Faulkner's late style, accounts of the Compson ancestors and brief surveys of the later lives of the novel's characters. Far from illuminating the novel, except in the interests of family chronicle and the retrospective purpose of Faulkner's design, it everywhere clashes with the novel, whose signal virtues create a world of timeless hallucination in which, when they are right, the words float lightly, silently through the novel's mysterious nets of consciousness, falling each into its ordered place.

The novel's appendix first appeared as a set piece in Malcolm Cowley's *The Portable Faulkner,* and Faulkner claimed then that, had he written it for the novel to begin with, "the whole thing would have fallen into pattern like a jigsaw puzzle when the magician's wand touched it." He also remarked, however, that it was "a piece without implications," and later, when challenged about its apparent contradictions to the novel, he replied that the inconsistencies prove "the book is still alive after 15 years, and being still alive is growing, changing." These confusing claims are entirely relevant to the larger problem of Faulkner's fictional design, in which novels simultaneously stand alone, contradict one another, or (it is said) fall into magic patterns from which no one piece of the puzzle could possibly be removed. Faulkner insisted that the appendix, when added to the novel, should appear at the beginning rather than the end (it has been published both ways) and described it at once as "the key to the whole book" and "an obituary." Analogously, the more he wrote—from *Absalom, Absalom!* on, say, after he had actually drawn a map of Yoknapatawpha—the more his fiction resembled new keys to the kingdom and a record of its creative decline toward death. Nowhere is this more apparent than in *Requiem for a Nun* (1951), where Faulkner attempts to extend the story of *Sanctuary*'s main attraction in the form of a play and indulges in long, cascading prose accounts of early Yoknapatawpha in which the ancestors of many of the characters and events of his fictional career appear in a patently legendary story of the Creation. Like the appendix to *The Sound and the Fury,* these accounts intertwine fine anecdotes and exceptionally bad writing, and they indicate how fragile and disordered the vision had become. But they also present a special kind of problem to readers: If the very essence of Faulkner's design is that it will remain incomplete, if the design (like that of Thomas Sutpen or the South itself) is flawed to start with, and if its whole development expresses a falling away from that which can never be reliably or precisely articulated, how then are works that claim such failures as virtues to be rejected?

The problem, of course, is not an imposing one: bad writing is bad writing, and some of Faulkner's is very bad indeed. It can be recognized as such, just as his great design, which will continue to attract encomiums and explication, can be ignored novel by novel. Yet the risk in ignoring it altogether, a risk *The Sound and the Fury* with its drummed-up appendix perfectly represents, is that the problems inherent in the greater design so resemble the problems with individual novels, and so much become part of their avowed thematic material, that one is left incapable of exact judgment if they are dismissed. There is little need now for more detailed analyses of the Faulkner canon or further exposés of his philosophical vision. The chapters that compose the second part of this study will take up social and historical contexts that are in need of more consideration: ones in which, to be precise, Faulkner becomes a great novelist. His explorations of the issues of race conflict and miscegenation, while they are implicit in earlier works, only come to the fore in and after *Light in August,* and one may justly divide his career in two, as I have done, recognizing one period to be devoted to a study of novelistic forms and the other to carrying those developed forms into a domain of greatest resonance. Moreover, *The Sound and the Fury,* as my reading of it will suggest, assumes just such a position of divided sensibility when one begins to examine its place in Faulkner's career.

There was not, of course, and there did not need to be any such strict division in Faulkner's own mind, and the latter portion of his career is in certain respects an extended, romantically failed attempt to deny that there were any disjunctions whatsoever. These kinds of characterizations may in any event seem somewhat arbitrary; others could be made and justified, but it needs to be emphasized, for example, how different *The Sound and the Fury* appears after it is put in the context of *Absalom, Absalom!* The powerful and instructive cross-references the later novel makes possible are what Faulkner's whole design depends on in more demanding ways; but leaving aside *The Unvanquished,* an addendum to *Sartoris* primarily of veiled autobiographical interest, and the sequential Snopes trilogy, this is the only instance where anything decisive or productive gets accomplished by comparison. In *Sanctuary,* to take a striking example, Faulkner's own revisions demonstrate that the novel, far from being ruined, is vastly improved by his discarding those sections that most connect the character of Horace Benbow to *Sartoris* and particularly its original version, *Flags in the Dust;* whereas *Requiem for a Nun,* at the opposite extreme, depends on *Sanctuary* and fragments of other novels to such an extent as to be a vacuous charade by itself. In this case and others, Faulkner's experimentation simply runs wild, as though its very purpose were to devise insurmountable dangers and create a context in which the strained forms and rhetorical excesses of earlier novels would appear to have been checked carefully at the point of utmost distention.

In this respect, the great design reproduces the structure of many individual novels, where characters and stories, however the plots may strive to entangle them, often seem to collide or to stand in taut juxtaposition; and while this method may produce superlative results at the contained, local level of the novel, its magnification through the span of a career makes the dubious virtues of disorder and conflict far too prominent. (What it also makes prominent is the apparent necessity of the design, for with the exception of *Soldiers' Pay,* the novels having little or nothing to do with Yoknapatawpha—*Mosquitoes, Pylon, The Wild Palms,* and *A Fable*—are also the least successful.) At extremity, as in *Go Down, Moses,* stories are nearly crushed together on the assumption that recurring themes and names, and the forces of rhetoric, can be made to dramatize their connection; and it is surely no coincidence that this novel marks by its precariously extenuated form the end of Faulkner's major work, as though his creative powers, after a final, draining surge, had broken under the pressures of the envisioned design. Like Cooper and Hawthorne before him, Faulkner set out to create a native American tradition, in his case by creating a whole country and people, and proceeded to do so on the modernist grounds prepared by Eliot and Joyce where tradition was a fabrication, a false and broken pattern of ruins. As these intentions became superimposed on the lost dream of the South, the design fell apart—what else could it do? And what could Faulkner do but continue adding to it, all the while assuring readers and critics that it was supposed to fall apart—what else could it do?

Despite such caveats, however, and despite his own cunning complicity in the authorial game of romantic failure, Faulkner wrote great fiction— the greatest when he wrote of the South as an explicit topic (as distinct from using it for regional atmosphere, which he always did) and, perhaps paradoxically, when his own anxieties about the value of the fictional forms he had chosen were most apparent. There is no doubt, to borrow from Martin Green's irreverent attack, that Faulkner produced "engines of mental torture, crucifixions of literary sensibility" (*Re-Appraisals: Some Common Sense Readings in American Literature*)—*The Sound and the Fury* is one of them—but he did so in a fashion that, at its better moments, created unseen worlds of unimagined words, and at its best perfectly accorded with the single most agonizing experience of his region and his nation: the crisis and long aftermath of American slavery. The formal explorations his finest early novels engaged in were preparation for things to follow, a search for a way to say things that had not been said but desperately needed saying, things that for good reason could barely be said. What he had to say is implicit in *The Sound and the Fury;* what is remarkable, and what constitutes the novel's central drama, is the difficulty he had in saying it at all.

Faulkner's achievement, as Robert Penn Warren has written, was foremost to articulate truths about the South and Southerners that had long been "lying speechless in their experience" and to confront turbulent issues that "would not have been available, been visible in fact, without the technique" he employed. This is certainly true, though it would only become visible some years after *The Sound and the Fury,* where what is speechless in the Southern experience nearly remains so and what is made available by Faulkner's technique is not immediately clear. Faulkner, however, had already articulated one dimension of the Southern experience, its contemporary estrangement from the heroic drama of the Confederate past, in *Sartoris*. The earlier novel anticipates many of Faulkner's themes and creates a number of characters that would reappear throughout his fiction. In particular, it anticipates a problem Faulkner would never fully resolve but, rather, would make the implied subject of all his work: that the estrangement of present from past is absolutely central to the Southern experience and often creates the pressured situation in which the past becomes an ever more ghostly and gloriously imposing model to the same extent that—like the childhood of a doomed, beautiful girl—it cannot be recaptured, relived, or even clearly remembered.

It is worth remarking in this regard that *Sartoris,* though it is not a great novel, is nonetheless emblematic of Faulkner's larger design as it explores the dilemma that is offered as the best possible evidence of the disjointed mind of the South: its inability to involve the spent dreams of the past with the pale realities of the present in dramatically convincing ways. In *Go Down, Moses* and *Intruder in the Dust* such failures of dramatic coherence and moral vision are so close to being the very material of the novels that arguments against them entail a certain risk; in this case, as in others, one must simply recognize the point at which mimetic disorder, in either moral or structural terms, destroys the coherence of the fictional design. In the case of *Sartoris,* the risk is a more peculiar one, for the same feature that makes the novel appear inadequate in its development, the missing or weakly characterized generations of the Sartoris family, is precisely what reveals the painful gap between the Civil War and World War I, between the wasted heroics of the first Sartorises and the suicidal courage of their descendants, and even—as it would turn out—between Faulkner's own early modernism and his gradual turning toward the materials of classic American fiction.

Beyond that, the original version, *Flags in the Dust,* was marred by excessive attention to the character of Horace Benbow and his incestuous attachment to his sister (a problem that would recur in the original version of *Sanctuary*). Faulkner's editor, Ben Wasson, complained that *Flags in the Dust* was six books in one—a charge that might also be leveled, say, at *Light in August* or *Go Down, Moses*—and set about the revisions that made *Sartoris* as good as it is. When Faulkner reflected on the novel and its revisions two years later, he began to speak of it in terms that only the work of the intervening years could have made possible:

> I realized for the first time that I had done better than I knew
> and the long work I had had to create opened before me and I

felt myself surrounded by the limbo in which the shady visions, the host which stretched half formed, waiting each with its portion of that verisimilitude which is to bind into a whole the world which for some reason I believe should not pass utterly out of the memory of man, and I contemplated those shady but ingenious shapes by reason of whose labor I might reaffirm the impulses of my own ego in this actual world without stability, with a lot of humbleness, and I speculated on time and death and wondered if I had invented the world to which I should give life or if it had invented me, giving me an illusion of greatness.

Aside from the botched prose and rather premature self-estimation, these remarks—almost mystically—allow a glimpse of the creative turmoil that did indeed seem to possess and invent Faulkner for over a decade after *Sartoris,* a period during which he worked off and on, as though "demon-driven," with the "insane fury" he would later say a writer requires. Although *Sartoris* is his most autobiographical novel, the world of the South that had truly "invented" Faulkner would only be recreated in bits and pieces, novel by novel, as successive personae and their families appeared. Over that period Faulkner would probe more deeply the limbo of "shady visions" from which he and his contemporary South had sprung; in *The Sound and the Fury,* written in part in the insane fury of his dejection over the problems and reception of *Sartoris,* he drove straight to the heart of that limbo but revealed only a suggestion of the shady visions it contained.

Even though the essay is a barely revised sketch, Faulkner's remarks on *Sartoris* suggest his fundamental cloudiness as a philosophical thinker; such ideas, of course, are not where his importance as a writer lies, and the novels most given to intellectual argument (*Mosquitoes, Intruder in the Dust,* parts of the Snopes trilogy, and *A Fable*) are striking disasters. Because *Sartoris* contains more able thinking about the dilemma of the South than any of his first major novels, however, it presents a peculiar point of departure for the work of the next ten or twelve years. On turning from *Sartoris* to *The Sound and the Fury* one feels, in effect, that thought has been declared impossible and ideas irrelevant, that "the mind of the South," which W. J. Cash later set out to define as a romantic continuum in a book by that name, rests rather, as C. Vann Woodward has observed of Cash, "on the hypothesis that the South has no mind" (*The Elusive Mind of the South*). There is some danger in approaching Faulkner from the perspective of Southern intellectual history, and, as the allusions to Faulkner among historians suggest, there is only one issue about which he has much to tell us: the issue of race and its many implied or visibly actual dilemmas, whose precise nature is that they can seldom be thought about clearly but instead leap instantly into the realm of hallucination. Of course there is good reason in this case to suggest that the *one* issue is *the* issue that determines and defines all others; and it is surely no mistake that Cash's *The Mind of the South* is most stridently powerful on the subjects of race hysteria and the correlative myth of a fallen aristocratic dream, just as Faulkner's most important novels revolve around the same subjects, for Cash and Faulkner are both romantics *manqué*—that is to say, severe critics of the romantic consciousness they feel most defines the essence of the South, to which they are enchantingly drawn and from which they recoil in horror.

While there is no doubt that *The Sound and the Fury* is troubled by deep underlying issues, the most perplexing thing about the novel is the discrepancy between its merits and the burdensome interpretations it has inevitably had to support. It is read as an allegory of the South, an exposition of the Oedipal complex, an ironic enactment of Christ's agony, and a sustained philosophical meditation on Time. While it engages all of these issues, it illuminates none of them very exactly; rather—and here lies part of its strange magnificence—it engages these issues, allows them to invade the domain of the novel's arcane family drama, and disavows their capacity to bring the novel out of its own self-enclosing darkness. The "psychology" that is of most interest in the novel is not Benjy's or Quentin's or Jason's or Dilsey's, but the psychology of the novel as a form of containing consciousness, one that is self-contained and at the same time contains, by defining in subliminal projection, Faulkner's most significant accomplishments and their ultimate derangement. There is more to be said of this psychology, but we may note again that the "mind" the novel does not have—and will not have until Faulkner's career develops—the mind of "the South," is paradoxically the only one that fully explains Quentin's incestuous fascination with Caddy's purity and the novel's strange obsession with her.

The Sound and the Fury begins in the mind of an idiot. Faulkner's detractors have suggested that once he discovered this impossible world he never left it, that Benjy Compson is, ironically, his one great creation, or, at best, that the novel is a fine modernist experiment unrivaled by following novels, in which Faulkner became obsessed with white Negroes and the like. This is at least half wrong, for *The Sound and the Fury* is not Faulkner's best novel, but the paradox is this: its importance only appears in the larger context of novels to which it gives rise, and at that point it comes to seem indispensable. Here again the question is genetic, so to speak, for the novel is demonstrably about failed integrity—in the Compson family, the Southern dream, the novel as a conventional form, and the "mind" of the author. All of these issues, rightly enough, appear to converge in the mind of Benjy, and the rest of the novel is a slow extraction of attention from this originating abyss. Such a narrative development produces paradoxical effects that bear on, and reappear in, all of Faulkner's work, but their most salient feature in this case is a thorough devaluation of traditional novelistic plot or action.

Nearly everything that "happens" in the novel happens in the first section—and this is exactly what Faulkner, who largely created for readers the idolatrous admiration of Caddy Compson they have expressed, asks us to believe. The genetic myth of the novel—that "it began with the picture of the little girl's muddy drawers, climbing that tree to look in the parlor window" at her grandmother's funeral—has so overwhelmed the novel itself that one no longer questions its relevance, even though there is good reason to do so. One might rather say that this scene stands in the same relation to Caddy as Caddy does to the entire novel, for we find out so little about her that we might conclude, on the basis of the action of the novel, either that she is a tender-hearted tramp or that, because she is surrounded by every conceivable form of mental and emotional instability, her own actions are justifiably inevitable. But since Caddy is not a character but an idea, an obsession in the minds of her brothers, we cannot rightly be said to find out much at all about her. Caddy is "lost" psychologically and aesthetically as well as morally: she is the very symbol of loss in Faulkner's world—the loss of innocence, integrity, chronology, personality, and dramatic unity, all the problematic virtues of his envisioned artistic design. To Benjy she smells like trees, to Quentin she is would-be lover, to Jason she is the whore mother of a whore daughter, and to Faulkner she is at once "the sister which I did not have and the daughter which I was to lose," and "a beautiful and tragic little girl" who later becomes, apparently, the mistress of a Nazi officer in occupied France. There is probably no major character in literature about whom we know so little in proportion to the amount of attention she receives. This is surely no objection to the novel, but it is quite certainly a measure of its drama, which is submerged to the point of invisibility.

Because the entire intent of *The Sound and the Fury* is to sequester modes of consciousness and formally depict them as incapable of responsive interaction, however, there may be no dramaturgical objection that can stand up on the grounds the novel presents. Its avowed strategy is to divide our attention among discrete modes of narrative revelation from which the novel's plot must be drawn over the course of several readings; once that is done—or even quite aside from it—we may then pay attention, respectively, to Benjy's libidinal creativity, Quentin's psychosis, Jason's satiric viciousness, or Dilsey's humble endurance. Holding together these discrete modes of narrative experience is the figure of the doomed girl; she lives in the formal vacuum of the novel, and in doing so she represents the still point, the "innocence" of mute action the four sections break away from as they dissolve into increasingly logical and coherent forms of narration. One has only to record the scene that Faulkner maintained was the heart of the novel—

> "All right." Versh said. "You the one going to get whipped.
> I aint." He went and pushed Caddy up into the tree to the first
> limb. We watched the muddy bottom of her drawers. Then we
> couldn't see her. We could hear the tree thrashing.

—to see how invisible Caddy truly is. Despite its marvelously elliptical portrayal of vanishing innocence and its vaguely erotic suggestion of something "dirty," this scene, without Faulkner's repeated insistence on its centrality, would itself vanish into the novel's larger pattern of glimmering memories.

If one were determined to choose any descriptive scene as central, surely either the muddying of those drawers or the wake of Caddy's deflowering or particularly her wedding (which formalizes those earlier events) would be more obvious:

> *In the mirror she was running before I knew what it was. That quick,*
> *her train caught up over her arm she ran out of the mirror like a cloud,*
> *her veil swirling in long glints her heels brittle and fast clutching her*
> *dress onto her shoulder with the other hand, running out of the mirror*
> *the smells roses roses the voice that breathed o'er Eden. Then she was*
> *across the porch I couldn't hear her heels then in the moonlight like a*
> *cloud, the floating shadow of the veil running across the grass, into the*
> *bellowing. She ran out of her dress, clutching her bridal, into the*
> *bellowing.*

Here, in this lyrical passage, is the wondrous center of the book—Caddy vanishing from the mirror of Quentin's narcissism into the wrenching, mindless vacuum of Benjy's bellowing: the death of Eden, Jefferson, April 1910; and the resurrection of the Edenic myth, Faulkner, 1929. But resurrection is yet to come (April 8, 1928): there is no rising without a fall, no fall without genesis, and it is eminently just, perhaps, that the scene

Faulkner grew enamoured of should appear, in the novel itself, no more consequential than others and vanish into the creative past of created loss. The genetic myth must remain mysterious, and its focal point must be projected as the one instant, the one spark that produces a whole world without necessarily resembling or defining it.

This peculiar and powerful dilemma goes to the heart of the novel, for the "loss" of Caddy (wherever one pinpoints it) represents the crucial generative event in the book—in fact, the event that forecloses generation. It is the moment of discovered grief that brings death, actual and metaphorical, into the psychological worlds of Benjy and Quentin; it is the moment of potential but elusive tragedy, envisioned deep within the novel's mind, from which the increasingly furious and distorted saga of the Compsons follows; and it is the catalytic moment of frightening disturbance that Faulkner would spend the better part of his career trying to recapture and define by transfiguring into ever more convulsive and historically searching dimensions. Each fragment of a scene devoted to the memory of Caddy is charged with a sure passion, at once moving and inadequate, that derives from the fragmentation of the narrative form itself, as though her figure were receding, reappearing, and receding again in the acts of remembrance that create her doomed, ethereal life. Those scenes together often constitute so fine and so troubling a memory, and so render in prose the poetry Faulkner had never found in verse, that we may forget that much of the novel—including many of the larger scenes in which those acts of memory are embedded—appears driven to madness in the further attempt to sustain their power in dramatic form and symbolic meditation. Caddy's story, as Faulkner leaves us to divine it (and, I will suggest, as his later fiction would reimagine it), is stunning. But it is also the novel's essential paradox that the small, certain beauties of Caddy's remembered fall should seem thoroughly at odds with the rhetorical fever and philosophical bewilderment that event produced in her family and her creator, while at the same time appearing to be their distant, irrevocable cause.

The last two sections of the novel may be said to suppress its greatest event altogether, for Caddy there becomes more and more marginal and eventually disappears altogether from the novel's conscious attention. Caddy is "the past" to the extent that she defines remembered moments that have been transfigured into disembodied hallucinations of lost love for Benjy and Quentin, and fierce hatred of his entire family for Jason; and as she is "past," so she is as dead as Mrs. Compson makes her by ordering that her name never be spoken in the house, and as dead as Jason treats her by embezzling her money and castigating her equally promiscuous daughter. With the possible exception of the bitterly peripheral Mrs. Compson, Jason is the novel's most brilliantly drawn character, and there is reason to feel that the same motives that later led Faulkner to put Caddy in the arms of a Nazi also led him to release his disgust with the family he had created in the restrained rage of Jason. Though he is conniving and corrupt, and though Faulkner and others have routinely spoken of him as a classic villain, Jason no doubt expresses every honest reader's response to the Compson family: "Blood, I says, governors and generals. It's a damn good thing we never had any kings and presidents; we'd all be down there at Jackson chasing butterflies." Without the edge of intimate hatred his narrative affords the novel, it would drift even further into psychological chaos and dramatic incoherence.

Yet the importance of Jason's section appears not simply in his brutal characterizations of his family—not, that is, in his lucid antipathy to their variously repelling personalities—but in the implied antipathy to the modes of narrative consciousness in which those personalities get presented. While Jason's wit forever fixes each of the novel's characters with penetrating sarcasm, its real value lies rather in its ability to reveal the necessity of a narrative consciousness that is capable—at last, it seems—of clear thought. Although his obsessions grow as well out of childhood betrayal, Jason's memories of the past are scant, and in each instance they lacerate those idealizations of unconscious frenzy the first two sections of the novel afford. His compulsive "I says," simmering with rage and maintaining the drive of his narration at a pace and a pitch furiously, mercenarily intent on making up for the lost time of childhood, stands in complete opposition to the chaotic first-person effusions of Benjy and Quentin; and his moral fervor, however disingenuous, immediately implies a reactionary aversion on Faulkner's part to the mindless riches of his first two central characters and to the claustrophobic forms of their narratives.

As though we were in danger of forgetting, Jason's pragmatic energy reminds us, among other things, that *The Sound and the Fury* is a novel, a fictional fabrication, and that despite Faulkner's apparent intentions it offers few philosophical ideas of lasting concern. When it does—in Quentin's speculations on time or Dilsey's experience of enduring salvation—it veers off into eccentricity at best, and at worst blooms into a grotesque caricature of its elementary symbolic structure: the death and resurrection of Christ. The novel is not an Easter vigil except by extraordinary sleight of hand or by sheer coincidence of dates. The Compsons inhabit the wasteland of Christian modernism Eliot had recently invented, to be sure, but this is scaffolding, not a stage; it is part of the novel's defunct mythology and has, with Faulkner's encouragement, become part of the myth of the novel. It is difficult to take seriously Quentin's memory of his father's teaching "that Christ was not crucified: he was worn away by a minute clicking of little wheels," or that "all men are just accumulations dolls stuffed with sawdust swept up from the trash heaps where all previous dolls had been thrown away the sawdust flowing from what wound in what side that not for me died not." And surely readers have only accepted the revival sermon of the "monkey" preacher in Dilsey's section because they are taken in by its pose of cathartic naturalism:

> And the congregation seemed to watch with its own eyes while the voice consumed him, until he was nothing and they were nothing and there was not even a voice but instead their hearts were speaking to one another in haunting measures beyond the need for words, so that when he came to rest against the reading desk, his monkey face lifted and his whole attitude that of a serene, tortured crucifix . . . Dilsey sat bolt upright, her hand on Ben's knee. Two tears slid down her fallen cheeks, in and out of the myriad coruscations of immolation and abnegation and time.

As the conclusion of this passage demonstrates, the problem here, as so often in Quentin's case, is not that the emotion of the scene is improbable but that its expressionistic contortions are made to bear an inconceivable burden, a symbolic weight far out of keeping with the novel's expressed inability to imagine and sustain such opaque philosophical ideas. The time-lessness of Dilsey's experience, the eschatological sublime of *Uncle Tom's Cabin,* validates the Christological structure of the plot only by declaring that, Negroes and idiots aside, it is of no real value whatsoever. Like the bloated, decaying bodies of Dilsey and Benjy with which we are confronted in the opening pages of section four, the book's typological vision, as though physically contorted by pressures originating deep within the mythical innocence of the book and of western civilization, inflates and bursts into dramatic parody and philosophical nonsense.

The more intently one examines any of the novel's philosophical positions or symbolic structures—most notably their correlative appearance in the ludicrous masque of the Passion—the more they reduce to seemingly unintentional parody or dissolve into a chaos of fragments. It could be argued that this is precisely the case, that the novel's strategy, in both dramatic and formal terms, is to portray a shattering of belief and to depict the urgent failure of modern consciousness to sustain any useful moral or temporal structures. One might then focus attention on the various symbolic patterns—mirrors, clocks, pear trees, Caddy, water, mud, fire, funerals, more clocks, the Easter apparatus—and declare the novel a vast prose poem, an interpretation of dreams, or an extended essay on *symbolisme*. As Hugh Kenner rightly points out, however, Faulkner's essential strategy (which he flamboyantly admitted on any number of occasions) "was not to symbolize (a condensing device) but to expand, expand," and his work characteristically "prolongs what it cannot find a way to state with concision, prolongs it until, ringed and riddled with nuance, it is virtually camouflaged by patterns of circumstance" (*A Homemade World: The American Modernist Writers*). Certainly, this is one of the primary effects of *The Sound and the Fury*, especially to the extent that the novel moves with deliberation from the static image-making capacity of Benjy's "mind" to increasingly conscious and compulsive first-person modes of narration, dwelling at last in the comparatively hyperbolic omniscience of the fourth section, where the crucifixion of the Compsons and the novel (and the reader) becomes most agonized. But it is just as certainly one of the novel's most paradoxical effects that, as it moves progressively out of its first frozen moments of lucid astonishment, a movement required to "tell the story," it also betrays its own proclaimed ideal and acquires the traits of bulging prose and crude, idiosyncratic symbolism Faulkner would become famous for, as though it were enacting its own deterioration and failure in the very course of getting the story told.

Another way to put this is to note that, once the plot of the novel is untangled, the first two sections give way almost entirely to similar but disconnected psychological and aesthetic problems. Benjy's section is compelling for the simple reason that it reduces the fictional vocabulary to a spare set of images that project, with kaleidoscopic accuracy, the whole "action" of the novel. Above all, his section is a masterpiece of controlled monotone, and its peculiar array of speech can only be construed as *interior dialogue*, for Benjy not only "says" nothing but can barely be said to think anything. The voices that appear, recollected at near random from some dozen enlightened moments of his existence, drop suspended into an area of consciousness that hauntingly resembles the pages of a novel, each act of speech punctuated by a full stop and a "said" almost without variation. It would not be unreasonable to suggest that Benjy is Faulkner's ideal narrator, the disembodied mode of consciousness he had in mind when he later told Malcolm Cowley that his method of composition was simply to "listen to the voices" and put down what they said, and that his desire (to borrow from a different context) was to "blue pencil everything which even intimates that something breathing and moving sat behind the typewriter which produced the books" (*Faulkner-Cowley File*). The narrative consciousness of Benjy mosaically projects (in memory) the "action" of *The Sound and the Fury,* and in this respect it also forecasts Faulkner's most persistent stylistic trait—composition by analogy, one detail or phrase suggesting another that resembles it, the second suggesting a third, the three brought into fortuitous dramatic alignment and swelling from within as though a whirlwind of rhetorical implications had grown from each seeded image.

This process is most obvious and most successful in *As I Lay Dying,* whose entire narrative containment, its limits as fragile and exact as the invisible boundaries of Benjy's mind, is a vacuum in which one "I said" after another, as it were, hangs suspended. Because both narratives are extended meditations on grief, on the fracturing of self into lost, discrete moments of memory, the resemblance between the perfections of control in Benjy's section and *As I Lay Dying* is no coincidence. More generally, one may see each of Faulkner's extrapolated formal experiments—in *Light in August, Absalom, Absalom!* or *Go Down, Moses,* for example—as developments of narrative as a form of containing "voices," in those later cases not simply voices as first-person utterances but rather as they expand under frenetic pressure into character, destiny, and obsession, whole stories hanging suspended in the perilous form of a novel as they recapitulate and refer to actions that are past, that are lost, that are dead, and have become the materials of prolonged elegy. In the cases of *Light in August* and *Absalom, Absalom!* and more particularly that of *Go Down, Moses,* the integrity of such form is tenuous in the extreme; stories not only arise by a method of analogical creation that virtually brings them into being at the moment they are required, but they also fuse with and "tell" one another's tales. As they are held at a point of merged and approximate conflict, the stories inhabit the form of the novel and absolutely determine it, in each instance complicating and extending the method Faulkner discovered in *The Sound and the Fury* of turning his novels into haunted chambers of consciousness, a discovery the anarchic arena of remembered voices in Benjy's section lucidly defines.

It is appropriate that Faulkner would later claim that in writing Benjy's section of the novel he had experienced an "emotion definite and physical and yet nebulous to describe . . . that ecstasy, that eager and joyous faith and anticipation of surprise which the yet unmarred sheets beneath my hand held inviolate and unfailing," for the disembodied narrative here accords speech by speech, syllable by syllable, with the strained but exacting forms of consciousness Faulkner's best work would require. In the other version of the introduction he associated that ecstasy more generally with the luminous image of Caddy in the pear tree; and he often claimed, of course, that he wrote her story four times without getting it right and gave up, and that none of his following novels allowed him to recapture the thrill of *The Sound and the Fury*. This too is part of the novel's myth, and one need not take it entirely seriously—except to note that the second attempt to tell Caddy's story, Quentin's section, often seems an anxious, enraged rehearsal of this view. Quentin's story is overrun by a vapid philosophizing that has elicited from readers the most regrettable kinds of attention. Quentin is, of course, both the sum of his Compson past and the sum of more and less recent literary pasts: like Stephen Dedalus, he is trapped in the nightmare of history (which in his case has as yet virtually nothing to do with history); and like Hamlet, moreover, Quentin is trapped in an obsession with incest (which in his case has as yet no clear bearing on the problems of the South or the novel, even though it appears to be at the center of both). *Absalom, Absalom!* will clarify these predicaments by giving Quentin and his novel a historical dimension of disturbing power. For the time being, however, Jefferson is neither Dublin nor Denmark, and the theme of incest slips lifelessly into obscure aesthetic fantasy.

One can measure the dangers of maturing the idiot narrator by comparing two passages in Quentin's section:

> I was running in the grey darkness it smelled of rain and all flowers scents the damp warm air released and crickets sawing away in the grass pacing me with a small travelling island of silence Fancy watched me across the fence blotchy like a quilt on a line I thought damn that nigger he forgot to feed her again I ran down the hill in the vacuum of crickets like a breath travelling across a mirror she was lying in the water her head on the sand spit the water flowing about her hips there was a little more light in the water her skirt half saturated flopped along her flanks to the waters motion in heavy ripples going nowhere renewed themselves of their own movement I stood on the bank I could smell the honeysuckle on the water gap the air seemed to drizzle with honeysuckle and with the rasping of crickets a substance you could feel on the flesh.

> The draft in the door smelled of water, a damp steady breath. Sometimes I could put myself to sleep saying that over and over until after the honeysuckle got all mixed up in it the whole thing

came to symbolise night and unrest I seemed to be lying neither asleep nor awake looking down a long corridor of grey halflight where all stable things had become shadowy paradoxical all I had done shadows all I had felt suffered taking visible form antic and perverse mocking without relevance inherent themselves with the denial of the significance they should have affirmed thinking I was I was not who was not was not who.

The one passage concerns Quentin's remembered painful encounter with Caddy after she lost her virginity; the other describes his—or rather, Faulkner's—extension of that trauma into the self-conscious domain of "ideas." The passages are entirely distinguishable, but they both move toward parodic inflation—in the first case introducing the erotic fantasy of murder and suicide with a knife Quentin proposes to Caddy, which leads in turn to the fantasy duel with Dalton Ames; and in the second hammering in the mock philosophy of Quentin's madness. The first passage, especially as it defines a line of subliminal action that suddenly erupts into Quentin's fight with Gerald Bland, as though the prose itself were waking from a dream, is the most brilliantly sustained part of Quentin's section. The second, however, takes the same germinal images in a direction unfortunately more representative of Quentin's character: a portrait of the artist as a young madman.

Quentin's section is altogether curious and perplexing. It contains beautiful, haunted writing that, as though to enact its own willed destruction, cannot resist drifting off into muddled self-examination; and we must be grateful for Faulkner's later admission that the preposterous conversation between Quentin and his father about incest with Caddy is imaginary, though we have then to admit the provocative—indeed, the crucial—probability that most all of Quentin's recollections, surely including many of his conversations with Caddy, are imaginary. It is not incidental that Quentin grows in part from a merger of the characters of Bayard Sartoris and Horace Benbow in *Flags in the Dust* and prefigures the clairvoyantly insane Darl Bundren in *As I Lay Dying,* for Quentin at this point is one of Faulkner's self-consciously insane aesthetes and has only the suggestion of those traits that lead from neurotic aestheticism to the nightmare of patrimonial grief as he later matures as a character in the Sutpen saga and, later still, develops even more fully in the character of Ike McCaslin. The most intriguing thing about the novel is that each of Faulkner's major works for the next fifteen years, from *As I Lay Dying* to *Go Down, Moses,* seems a more complex and powerful reworking of material that would in retrospect appear hidden beneath the surface of Quentin's dilemma, largely unconscious and invisible, as it were, but nonetheless capable of arousing turbulent and creative emotions that Faulkner, at this point, cannot fully articulate. In this respect, the greater context of his career may be said virtually to create the significance of *The Sound and the Fury;* and far from failing to measure up to its high standard, his later novels, particularly *Absalom, Absalom!* and *Go Down, Moses,* probe and define the historical and psychological depths of the Compson tragedy in ways that are much more illuminating than either Faulkner's appendix or his romantic pronouncements of succeeding artistic failures could suggest.

Even so, the shadows of Faulkner's tragic world are here, and an extraordinary passion, physical and intellectual, lies hidden in this book and haunts this pair of failed sons and fathers. To speak of Mr. Compson and Quentin in this way is appropriate not least because their conversations, which approach and dwell in the *imaginary* whether or not we conceive of them as actually taking place, embody in their reduction to ridiculous romantic symbolism and whispers of gallantry the failure of a land, a people, a family—all of them known together as "the South"—to regenerate itself. Mr Compson's cynical disinterest in Caddy's promiscuity and Quentin's narcissistic obsession with it represent, not opposing views, but views that are complementary to the point of schizophrenia: the father having renounced passion and patrimony altogether, the son attempting psychically to totalize it, to invest an entire family and its cultural role in an imaginary act of incest. The absence of Caddy as a character and the fantastic character of Quentin's passion are in this respect entangled, even indistinguishable, for the incestuous desire to father oneself or to be one's own family is here presented as correlative to, if not the cause of, the symbolic desire to absorb all creative energy into an invisible, ineffable presence—what is present only as desire, that perfect form into which all energy is channeled, all content sublimated, the vaselike erotic form Faulkner imagined his book itself to be.

Quentin's suicide, therefore, should not be interpreted as a reaction against his incestuous desires or their failure to be actualized; rather, his suicide, like that of Melville's hero in *Pierre,* virtually *is* incest, the only act in which generation is thoroughly internalized (and prohibited) and the "father," as a consequence, killed. Here the rage that everywhere fractures the family and the book, the hatred of his past Quentin will deny in *Absalom, Absalom!* (or has already denied, if we merge the events of the two books), is folded into the act of love, in the bodily *image* of love: Quentin joins the water, the medium always associated with Caddy, as though he were lying down with it (one thinks of Millais's *Ophelia*), his bodily self falling to meet the enchanted corpse lying always beneath the shadowy surface of the prose. Death and love, murder and passion, are joined in incest, most of all in such an imaginary enactment and its sublimation in suicide. Quentin's death, of course, is offstage, just as invisible, in our experience of the novel, as Caddy herself; this is perfectly to the point, however, for as his reappearance in *Absalom, Absalom!* and the original stories of *Go Down, Moses* will suggest, Quentin's death, like his proscribed desires, is also *imaginary,* a symbolic distillation of the moral suicide diffused in later novels through the trauma of the Civil War, Reconstruction, broken promises, the failure of freedom and love—the encompassing drama that surrounds and defines for Faulkner the central act of grief.

The risks of such an aesthetic, one in part created retrospectively by the directions in which Faulkner was to take his initial impulses, are evident in *The Sound and the Fury,* a novel whose very essence is imaginary in that the "plot" or "story" is of almost no consequence but remains instead a way to project into actuality the inchoate states of grief and unfulfilled desire that are Faulkner's abiding subjects. Like Benjy's broken flower, his dirty slipper, and his fire, the story—by extension, the novel itself, as Faulkner would have it—is at once a memorial and a fetish; as it embodies loss without adequately containing or reproducing it, the story gets progressively more full and realistic in a traditional sense but cannot find an expression equivalent or superior to Benjy's opening inarticulate cry of Caddy's name. In the final image of Benjy circling the Confederate statue we recognize that, although the plot has unfolded and advanced, its essence still lies in section one, to which we nervously return. The returning to stillness, as to death, is the book's primary movement, and the style of Benjy's section, stillness on the point of death, enacts in narrative the hard, bright flame of symbolic intensity that Quentin imagines incest to be, and Faulkner wanted his book to be, the burning out in passionate stillness of the power to generate a family, a life, a story.

From a therapeutic point of view, if no other, it is quite plausible to maintain, as Maxwell Geismar does, that the novel speaks in accents "from the edge of the womb" that "recall and draw up from the abyss of the past our own forgotten memories" (*Writers in Crisis: The American Novel, 1925–1940*); and the novel is surely, as David Minter suggests, a central point of departure among Faulkner's "strategies for approaching forbidden scenes, uttering forbidden words, committing dangerous acts" (*William Faulkner: His Life and Work*). The disjunction between these virtues and the novel's philosophical and rhetorical excess is a rather considerable one, however, and the greater one's attention to this disjunction, the more the novel resembles the Southern aesthetic predicament Faulkner spoke of in one version of his suppressed introduction: "In the South art, to become visible at all, must become a ceremony, a spectacle; something between a gypsy encampment and a church bazaar given by a handful of alien mummers who must waste themselves in protest and active self-defense until there is nothing left with which to speak." On a more positive note, Faulkner spoke in the other version of having learned to read, as though "in a series of delayed repercussions," his literary masters, "the Flauberts and Dostoievskys and Conrads." This is exciting but somewhat spurious (it would, no doubt, have been indiscreet to add Eliot and Joyce, whom he had more obviously been learning to read); the important readings by repercussion would only come later, when Faulkner reread *The Sound and the Fury*, so to speak, and became his own literary master.

Faulkner's obsession with the unnameable, the inexpressible, is his own greatest hazard, and *The Sound and the Fury* is its most intricate expression. As it forecasts his preoccupation with form rather than plot, with modes of conflicting, antagonistic expression that depend on abrupt juxtaposition, sheer rhetorical energy, and exhaustive symbolic motifs, the novel embodies an incipiency of method that accords with its infantile accents and forbidden scenes. Still, it is difficult to tell why—or exactly at what point—its poignant memories get transfigured into neurosis or bizarre, overbearing symbolism. It quite often appears to have little to do with its own genetic myth, the image of Caddy in the pear tree that Faulkner claimed was "the only thing in literature which would ever move me very much," even though it can easily be reduced to that image. Its interests remain largely unconscious, not just in the sense of intimating deep psychoanalytic drama, but also in the sense of deriving their power everywhere from such simple, abiding images, which as the novel tells us time and again are distorted and betrayed when they mature into stories. As Faulkner was fond of remarking, he wrote the "story" four times and gave up without getting it right. That, of course, is the novel's central myth; but it is worth considering, in the larger context of Faulkner's most important work—a context that has helped to create the myth—one reason why he could not get it right, why its interests may most be said to be unconscious, and why the obsession with Caddy was no mistake.

Clearly, the novel is about the doom of the South, but only *Absalom, Absalom!* provides the explosive historical setting in which this is fully evident. And as John Irwin has demonstrated, only an imposed strategy of assumptions about the nature of familial and temporal revenge can explicate

Quentin's "ideas" at all. That pattern, Irwin argues, is put into perspective by the larger tragedy of Thomas Sutpen's family, which in retrospect—or rather, by an act of retrospection that is intimately involved with the desire for revenge—illuminates Quentin's suicide by proving to him, as it were, that it truly is a repetition of past doomed actions, just as his desire for Caddy is a repetition of past frustrated desires. Because he comes to realize that tragedy *is* repetition and that its deepest level, in this case, lies in the "symbolic identification of incest and miscegenation," it may be said that Quentin's obsession with Caddy's virginity is determined by forces that exist even further beneath the nether reaches of consciousness that a good portion of *The Sound and the Fury* dwells in, forces that only the historical depth of *Absalom, Absalom!* can reveal. As Irwin points out, Quentin's attempt "to avenge his sister's lost virginity (proving thereby that it had once existed) and maintain the family honor is an attempt to maintain . . . the possibility of the existence of a virgin space within which one can still be first, within which one can have authority through originality." But the most tormenting denial of that virgin space, at the level of cultural history the second novel adds to the first, lies in the fact that "the Civil War closed off the virgin space and the time of origins, so that the antebellum South became in the minds of postwar Southerners that debilitating 'golden age and lost world' in comparison with which the present is inadequate."

This dimension of the Compson tragedy is dramatically "repressed" in 1929, however, and the larger importance of Irwin's reading of the novel's interior myth must necessarily be pursued in the context of *Absalom, Absalom!,* in which one might argue that the issue of miscegenation, which Irwin constantly alludes to, is even more important than he claims; that it is more central to Quentin's dilemma than the problematic of Oedipal revenge. At this point, Faulkner seems as much stymied by the theme of incest as Quentin is by his futile desire to avenge Caddy's violation. If Quentin's obsession with Caddy's purity is to move beyond the emotional lassitude and moral paralysis that William Taylor has found to characterize the personality of the "Southern Hamlet" (*Cavalier and Yankee*), it will have to engage something like the shock produced by the intrusion of modern morality into the closed cult of Southern sentimentality—the shock produced, for example, when the dissipated college youth of the Prohibition era, as Cash suggests, confronted his own puritanical heritage:

> This bawdy outburst struck straight against Southern Puritanism
> and sentimentality—particularly the cult of Southern Woman-
> hood—and so served to add to the sum total of fears on its own

account. . . . For in the bottom of the minds of even the most flauntingly "emancipated" of these youths, the old sentimentality and Puritanism bred in their bones from youth still lurked, and often started up to torture the young woman with longing for the old role of vestal virgin, the young man with longing for the old gesturing worship of a more than mortal creature— to make them continually restless with the subconscious will to escape into being nearly whole again.

It will be the burden of Faulkner's career to develop a rationale for the South's paralysis and its resulting resurgence of sentimental longing. The nadir of the shock of modernism, and its blasphemous inversion, Faulkner probes in *Sanctuary*, where the promiscuity of Caddy turns into the wild nymphomania of Temple Drake and the purity of Southern Womanhood becomes a pornographic farce—and where, moreover, Faulkner disgorges himself in mockery of his own initial psychoanalytic aestheticism. But the greatest shock he would save for *Light in August, Absalom, Absalom!,* and *Go Down, Moses.* There the shock comes in the abundantly evident bearing the threat of miscegenation has on Southern gynealotry and, we may surmise, on Quentin's incestuous desires.

In *The Sound and the Fury,* however, it is precisely this issue that is left inarticulate; and the most significant and tragic dimension of Southern narcissism Faulkner would later explore—the hallucinating, self-projected image of "the Negro" that the South created out of guilt and fear, the image so wonderfully and shockingly embodied in the monstrous, uncanny figures of the "white niggers," Joe Christmas and Charles Bon—lies speechless in Quentin's experience. In this instance as well as others one feels the force of Irving Howe's contention that there is nowhere in Faulkner's work "a copious and lively image of the old South. It remains forever a muted shadow, a point of reference rather than an object for presentation, perhaps because the effort to see it in fullness would be too great a strain on the imagination." The shadow of the old South, and most obviously the shadow of "the Negro" it carries in forbidding proximity, are *in retrospect* (as Irwin argues) everywhere visible in the "shadow" self Quentin pursues and, finally, kills. By the time Faulkner's readers would be in a position to make such an assertion, though, the imaginative strain would have become so intense that Quentin's psychosis might well seem the best measure of Faulkner's painstakingly created design and his suicidal narcissism a mirror of the South's long-defeated dream.

Such a strategy is precarious and, to repeat, it only becomes visible over the course of Faulkner's career. Yet the shock produced by the intrusion of the modern into the domain of Southern puritanism and the Southern cult of memory is already evident in *Sartoris,* where the paralyzing disjunction between the new Sartorises and the old is sharply rendered by the novel's ability to hold the myth of memory at a point of perilous balance, neither endorsing it nor declaring it sheer fabrication. In doing so, it brings into view the most conspicuous feature of Faulkner's romantic mythologizing of the old South—that its power depends on his straining to the very limits of coherence those nostalgic legends of old Confederate times that were being offered up in all seriousness by his contemporaries. What one witnesses over the course of Faulkner's career is the increasing irrationality of the claims made on behalf of the old South as the new South approached the disillusioning realities of black civil rights activism and legislation, an irrationality for which his tortuous prose becomes a mirror but which also produces the bewildering effect that, the more Faulkner probes the myth, the more central it becomes, while the more he confronts its visceral elementary issue—the hallucinating figure of "the Negro"—the more he recoils into a form of outrage that is ambivalent in the extreme. By the time of his notorious public stands on desegregation in the 1950s, that ambivalence would come to seem painful indeed, and would seem as well to represent a retreat from the explosive moral stands his novels had already taken.

In *The Sound and the Fury,* then, incest is made to stand for something larger than itself, something having to do with the doom of "the South," but something we will not read of very explicitly until the early pages of *Absalom, Absalom!,* in which Mr. Compson remarks to Quentin, "Years ago we in the South made our women into ladies. Then the War came and made the ladies into ghosts." The ghost-lady here is Rosa Coldfield, whose withering erotic fantasies seem to embody all that Judith and Ellen Sutpen are not allowed to say in the novel and, moreover, all that Quentin, perhaps, comes to think Caddy capable of saying if only she were allowed, by Faulkner, to say it. In between the two novels, Faulkner attributes versions of Caddy's suppressed confessions to Temple Drake and Joanna Burden, whose nymphomania—in each case prompted by her sexual violation by a "black man"—represents that underlying horror the revelation of which Quentin would prevent (and enact as surrogate) by enclosing his sister and himself in a state of damned, Pateresque purity: *"If it could just be a hell beyond that: the clean flame the two of us more than dead. Then you will have only me then only me then the two of us amid the pointing and the horror beyond the clean flame."* Quentin's incestuous desires do, no doubt, define a libidinal

Oedipal drama played out among the Compsons, father and son and preceding generations (we may later propose on the basis of the appendix),
but this drama is argued and not acted by the novel; as of yet it has not
completely engaged the central tragedy of the South and is more discon-
certing than T. S. Eliot found Hamlet's problems to be. At best, it remains
the aesthetic problem it had been for Horace Benbow, that unfathomable,
transgressive state of artistic perfection with which Faulkner himself had
been preoccupied from the beginning of his career and that was now being
passed through the furnace of Quentin's mind to reappear transfigured into
more daring and dangerous forms in succeeding novels as the lost story of
lost Caddy went on being told.

The Sound and the Fury is an apt title in more ways than one, for as
Faulkner's remarks on the writing of Sartoris suggest, a creative convulsion
of immense magnitude takes place between the two novels, as though
Faulkner has entered the dream world, the limbo, that would make available
his greatest materials. The new novel screens from view its most significant
effects (for they have not yet been created); it also screens Sartoris by dissolving the linear structures of history, family, and the novel, and leaving
a residue of first-person obsessions, fragments of identity that reach beyond
the ghostly forms of consciousness that contain them but, touching nothing
and no one, remain segregated and irreconcilable. Most significantly, in
view of Faulkner's later development, they do little to touch the issues of
race in which he would amplify those distortions and failures of sexual,
generative power he had here found to constitute the crisis of Southern
identity. The black characters in The Sound and the Fury do provide a context
for the social and psychic decay of the Compsons, and that context is crucial;
but as the marginal attention given to them in the appendix suggests, it
would not be evident until Light in August why, as Quentin observes to
himself, a "nigger" is not a person but "a form of behaviour; a sort of
obverse reflection of the white people he lives among." At that point,
Quentin's obsession with Caddy's purity acquires a more subtle and provocative coherence, for the introduction of the theme of miscegenation
reveals the absolute paradox in his obsession. Because the etymology and
received meaning of incest suggest precisely the opposite, such purity is
blasphemous by definition: incest is impure. To recognize this does not
significantly change our perspective on Quentin's fantasy in Oedipal terms.
It does, however, begin to alter Caddy's position as representative embodiment of Southern virtue and as ghostly echo of an honored ideal under
severe contemporary pressures; and it begins to clarify why Quentin, as
the Appendix would put it, "thought he loved but really hated in her what

he considered the frail doomed vessel of [his family's] pride and the foul instrument of its disgrace."

Quentin's madness, as Faulkner came to depict it and as the retrospective vantage of the appendix could more justly assume, is primarily the South's, whose intense fascination with gynealotry increased in proportion to threats against it and created the peculiar situation in which the period of Southern history that came mythically to embody extreme virtue and honor, the antebellum years, was precisely the period whose virtue and honor, however they may have been manifested, were built on the most hideous corruptions of the human spirit imaginable. Like Quentin's conception of incest, such nostalgic conjuring makes "pure" what is thoroughly "impure"—though with this important complication: because incest defines a violation of purity or caste (*in* + *castus*), the integrity of the antebellum South, since it was projected in direct opposition *against* the violent threat of miscegenation that abolition and emancipation were said to entail, might well seem a clean, pure space of remembered innocence. Mr. Compson's contention that Caddy's purity is a "negative state" defined only by violation (a contention repeated in more complex form in *Absalom, Absalom!*) or that it is "like death: only a state in which the others are left" (a contention *Absalom, Absalom!* seems designed to illustrate) is thus to the point: Caddy's purity and that of the South are defined by a transgression or violation of moral limits that virtually brings them into being, that define what is just as irrevocably lost, past, and "dead" as Caddy herself. Quentin's dilemma is to imagine that by committing the act himself he can preserve that purity by defining it in violation, much as the ideal poet (or the novelist obsessed with "unmarred" and "inviolate" sheets of paper) might preserve aesthetic purity in the consuming sacrificial flame of creation without properly generating anything except the perfect, sacred, unreadable utterance.

If it is to act thus in counterpoint to Quentin's obsessions, Caddy's moral fragility, like her near invisibility as a character, must be seen to portray the violent paradox upon which such conceptions of Southern innocence were built. This paradox would seem irrelevant to (or entirely at odds with) the issue of miscegenation if the contemporary fear of sexual mixing between blacks and whites did not entail a willful denial that Southern innocence, symbolized by its essential purity of white blood, had not already been irrevocably lost. As his work revealed, when Faulkner turned from *Light in August*'s shocking exposure of the Jim Crow rape complex to the sins of the fathers that had set it in motion in *Absalom, Absalom!* and *Go Down, Moses*, this idealizing myth of innocence required the unconscious repression or deliberately conscious suppression of the miscegenation of white masters and black slaves, which not only counted for little or nothing in terms of human love but also made conceivable forms of incest that paradoxically could not be defined as such since the intimate family relationships incest assumes were, by further definition, declared utterly invalid. The transferral of threatened sexual violence to emancipated blacks revealed the idolatry of Southern womanhood, in part, as a feverish sublimation of the lust of white masters for their slave women, a lust that could only be condoned by the insistence that it had no moral or emotional content but, because it inevitably did, therefore insured the ostentatiously proclaimed sanctity of white women and white marriage. In retrospect, that sublimation would be more severe than ever, for the logic of emancipation, in sexual terms as in others, created the specter of terrifying revenge, a specter far more monstrous than the actualization of such revenge would ever be.

By the time Faulkner began his literary career, the "lost" but feverishly maintained innocence of the South, so like Quentin's paradoxically puritanical concept of Caddy's purity, had become nothing less than the entire burden of white identity, and the threat against it was more and more obviously constituted, as Joel Williamson has noted, by the failure of "the myth of the mulatto demise." The historically prevalent Southern view that mulattoes were a dying breed, both biologically and culturally, and that the sins of the antebellum fathers were therefore passing from view, had begun to be exposed as a myth in its own right by the early twentieth century, with the result that miscegenation, whether instigated by whites or blacks, came to seem more heinous and the purity of white women more crucial than ever. "To merge white and black would have been the ultimate holocaust, the absolute damnation of Southern civilization," Williamson writes, and yet the mulatto made apparent "that white and black had interpenetrated in a graphic and appalling way," that "life in the Southern world was not [as] pure, clean, and clear as white people needed to believe" (*New People: Miscegenation and Mulattoes in the United States*).

This interpenetration of the races need not, of course, require us to believe in the thorough interpenetration of either the twin themes of incest and miscegenation or the two novels those themes bring into troubled union. At this point they do not, in Faulkner's imagination, belong together as explicitly as *Absalom, Absalom!* will insist, and one need not believe that the threat of miscegenation is the repressed fear generating Quentin's incestuous desire in order to witness, as Faulkner's career unfolds, the absorption of a private, aesthetic neurosis by a potentially more volatile, comprehensive cultural disorder. That disorder, the threat to the fragile innocence of the white South, along with the historical dimension of tragic action it implies, is latent in *The Sound and the Fury* in the same way that the entirety of Quentin's tormented involvement in the conclusion of the Sutpen saga may be said to be latent, as if by imaginary projection, in the events of June 2, 1910. Miscegenation promised the slow but eventual extinction of the white race (few bothered to notice that the contrary might also be true); like incest, its exact opposite in the operation of prohibitions, it meant the suicidal failure of families and their caste to be perpetuated. It also meant the lasting extinction of a memory, a dream, in which half the South (and the nation) lived in an illusion, the other half in the long shadow it cast.

This complex situation, which Faulkner came to see as the heart of the South's damnation, in all its related mythical and contemporary extenuations, is left broodingly unconscious in *The Sound and the Fury,* which we only recognize at all in the larger context of later novels, where its shadow looms up in monstrous proportions. There is virtually no way to read it out of the novel itself, even though it adds a dimension of exceptional power to Quentin's theatrical agony; it is, so to speak, one of the novel's myths—paradoxically its most crucial and speechless. It is surely no mistake, however, that Faulkner some years later would burlesque Quentin's obsession with Caddy by describing his concept of honor as "the minute fragile membrane of her maidenhead," as precariously balanced as "a miniature replica of all the whole vast globy earth may be poised on the head of a trained seal," and then in the same vein of wretched prose describe Jefferson itself, and the anecdote it here produced, circa 1864, as "a bubble, a minute globule which has its own impunity" but which was also "too weightless to give resistance for destruction to function against . . . having no part in rationality and being contemptuous of fact." The myth at the heart of *The Sound and the Fury* was as weightless and intangible (and as subject to grotesque caricature) as the lost dream it depended on. Nothing that Faulkner was to write would prove it otherwise, but he would certainly find better and more dramatically exacting ways to say it.

Sartre's essay on *Sartoris,* though not as well known as his essay on *The Sound and the Fury,* is at once more penetrating and more capable of defining the peculiar relationship of the two novels as complementary points of origin in Faulkner's career. The "real drama" of Faulkner's work, says Sartre in passing from the particular case of *Sartoris* to a more general characterization of Faulkner's world, lies "*behind,* behind the lethargy, behind the gestures, behind the consciousness." His imposing tragic figures, Sartre points out, have only "exterior dimension" despite the obvious emphasis on their interior chaos; they have "secrets" that can neither be revealed nor "forced back into the unconscious," and Faulkner therefore "dreams of an absolute obscurity in the very depth of the 'conscious,' of a complete obscurity that we should ourselves create within ourselves." These observations are entirely more instructive than Sarte's famous meditations on "time" in *The Sound and the Fury;* for the "conscious obscurity" of which Faulkner is master refers to both a method and a locale, and in the case of the transition from *Sartoris* to *The Sound and the Fury* perfectly describes the move away from a clear articulation of the Southern myth and toward its gothic complication in later works, where his expression of both the mind and the manner of the South is far from unconscious but engages instead the consciously created obscurity that is both the South's mind and our own American "self."

The shadow of "the Negro," because its capacity to figure an unconscious eruption, the sudden return of the repressed, is so powerful, magnificently marks this boundary for Faulkner; and his career up to *Light in August* might well be considered an extended repression of the figure of the Negro, who truly remains a *figure* for Faulkner since his great "black" characters are "white." But that novel, along with *Absalom, Absalom!* and *Go Down, Moses,* reveals a new depth of consciousness that is violent and haunting, that certainly has the characteristics of a gothic nightmare, but ought not, insofar as Faulkner's narratives are explicitly composed of formal modes of fictional consciousness, be considered "unconscious." That is to say, the depth of racial consciousness those novels engage is of explosive social, rather than strictly psychoanalytic, interest. On the other hand, as *Absalom, Absalom!* would prove in detail, *The Sound and the Fury* does force this central issue back into the unconscious, for there is almost nothing in the earlier novel—while there is everything in the later novel—to indicate that miscegenation or its shadowy threat is an important feature of Quentin's psychological disturbance. One might say that *The Sound and the Fury,* in this respect, *contains* the repressed that returns with increasing visibility over the course of Faulkner's career as he discovers the lost dimension of Southern experience *Sartoris* had failed to find. It is truly unconscious at this point, as though (we recognize in retrospect) Faulkner were passing toward the "depths of consciousness" through a melodrama of Southern family romance that cannot yet reveal its most peculiar and definitive secret.

More particularly, he was moving away from the autobiographical dilemma that *Sartoris* bogged down in; and while it is possible and quite profitable to detect recurring familial dramas throughout Faulkner's work that resemble his own in striking ways, and while a number of his characters may be seen as authorial personae, the glimmers of autobiography left in

The Sound and the Fury, in contrast to *Sartoris,* are tellingly marginal. Genealogical conflict has been compressed into a measured disintegration and restoration of temporality, and history has momentarily disappeared into the stalemate of psychoanalytic compulsion; but Faulkner seems also to have entered a cauldron of creativity and produced, in a white heat of experimental expression, the precipitous materials and their strained, immature forms that would allow him to write great novels. The most vital myth of *The Sound and the Fury*—one that we can neither rely upon nor confidently gainsay—is that it made possible everything else. His next creative efforts would produce a recasting of the materials of the Southern wasteland into the bitter and hateful denunciations of *Sanctuary,* and a perfectly tuned and controlled essay on forms of grief in *As I Lay Dying;* while each of his great novels that follow would refer back implicitly or explicitly to *The Sound and the Fury,* as intimately but tenuously connected to it as the novel is to its own germinal scene and its central, invisible character. The book is its own myth, as the design of Faulkner's career came to define it, a myth of tortured innocence explicated by earlier and later novels but at the same time self-contained and—intentionally, it seems—self-defeating.

It would, perhaps, be too much to speak of the novel as a kind of womb or genesis, for its avowed depictions of luminously failed beginnings, as well as the novel's accumulated myth of ecstatic purity, suggest that nothing could ever come of it or surpass it, that is is perfectly stillborn. This is certainly not true, and Faulkner's later comparison of the novel to a "child who is an idiot or born crippled" is more to the point. Like Quentin's notion of incest, the myth of the novel's perfection is half bombast and hallucination, but its importance is literally inestimable, for the simple reason that "Faulkner" can be imagined apart from it no more easily than the novel can be imagined apart from Caddy, "the beautiful one, [his] heart's darling." It contains brilliant, powerful writing that Faulkner would publically declare to be his best, writing that could, therefore, never be equalled. As though visibly enacting his own "compulsion to say everything in one sentence," and inevitably failing to do so, *The Sound and the Fury* defines his vision and its uttermost limits. It also contains the inchoate drama of the South that would mature into his best work over the course of the next decade. By the time Faulkner added the novel's appendix, that work would be several years behind him; and the design of Yoknapatawpha, obsessively recapitulating and shoring up earlier works, would more and more resemble the chaos from which it had sprung—with the paradoxical effect, of course, that only the furthering of the design could define its latent, magnificent failure and fix forever the myth of its original masterpiece.

Chronology

1897	Born William Cuthbert Falkner, in New Albany, Mississippi, on September 25; first child of Murry Falkner, then a railroad executive, and Maud Butler.
1914	Leaves school after long history as a poor student.
1916–17	Lives on fringe of student community at the University of Mississippi.
1918	Tries to enlist in U.S. armed forces, but is refused. Works in New Haven, Connecticut, for Winchester Gun factory. Changes spelling of name from "Falkner" to "Faulkner." Enlists in Canadian Air Force, but war ends while he is still in training.
1919	Returns to Oxford and enters the University of Mississippi. Writes poems that will be included in *The Marble Faun*.
1920	Leaves the university, but remains in Oxford.
1921	After spending autumn in New York City, returns to Oxford to work as postmaster.
1924	Resigns postmastership; *The Marble Faun*.
1925–26	New Orleans period, frequently in circle surrounding Sherwood Anderson. Writes *Soldiers' Pay* and *Mosquitoes;* travels to Europe and resides in Paris; returns to Oxford.
1927	Writes *Flags in the Dust*, which is rejected.
1928	Writes *The Sound and the Fury*.
1929	*Sartoris* (curtailed version of *Flags in the Dust*) published. Marriage of Faulkner and Estelle Franklin on June 20. Finishes *Sanctuary;* publishes *The Sound and the Fury;* begins *As I Lay Dying*.
1930	Finishes and publishes *As I Lay Dying;* revises *Sanctuary*.
1931	Daughter Alabama is born in January and dies the same month. *Sanctuary* published; begins *Light in August*.

1932   Finishes *Light in August,* which is published after his father's death; begins first Hollywood screenwriting period.

1933   *A Green Bough;* daughter Jill born.

1934   *Doctor Martino and Other Stories.*

1935   *Pylon.*

1936   *Absalom, Absalom!*

1938   *The Unvanquished.*

1939   *The Wild Palms.*

1940   *The Hamlet.*

1942   *Go Down, Moses.*

1946   *The Portable Faulkner.*

1948   *Intruder in the Dust.*

1949   *Knight's Gambit.*

1950   *Collected Stories;* Nobel Prize in literature.

1951   *Requiem for a Nun.*

1954   *A Fable.* First assignment for State Department.

1955   Goes to Japan for State Department.

1957   *The Town.*

1959   *The Mansion.*

1960   Faulkner's mother dies.

1962   *The Reivers.* Faulkner dies in Byhalia, Mississippi, on July 6, from coronary occlusion.

Contributors

HAROLD BLOOM, Sterling Professor of the Humanities at Yale University, is the author of *The Anxiety of Influence, Poetry and Repression*, and many other volumes of literary criticism. His forthcoming study, *Freud: Transference and Authority*, attempts a full-scale reading of all of Freud's major writings. A MacArthur Prize Fellow, he is general editor of five series of literary criticism published by Chelsea House. During 1987–88, he served as Charles Eliot Norton Professor of Poetry at Harvard.

JOHN T. IRWIN has written *Doubling and Incest/Repetition and Revenge, American Hieroglyphic*, and a volume of poetry, *The Heisenberg Variations*. Formerly editor of the *Georgia Review*, he now teaches at Johns Hopkins University and directs the Writing Seminars.

DONALD M. KARTIGANER teaches at the University of Washington, Seattle. Besides *The Fragile Thread: The Meaning of Form in Faulkner's Novels*, he has edited, along with Malcolm A. Griffith, *Theories of American Literature: The Critical Perspective*.

GARY LEE STONUM teaches at Case Western Reserve University and has written *Faulkner's Career: An Internal Literary History*.

WARWICK WADLINGTON teaches at the University of Texas, Austin, and is the author of *The Confidence Game in American Literature*.

THADIOUS M. DAVIS is a recipient of the Pushcart Prize in Poetry and is poetry editor of *Black American Literature Forum*. Author of *Faulkner's "Negro": Art and the Southern Context*, she teaches at the University of North Carolina, Chapel Hill.

JOHN T. MATTHEWS has written on Faulkner and Brontë. He is Professor of English at Boston University.

GAIL L. MORTIMER teaches at the University of Texas, El Paso, and is the author of *Faulkner's Rhetoric of Loss: A Study in Perception and Meaning.*

ERIC J. SUNDQUIST teaches at the University of California, Berkeley. Besides *Faulkner: The House Divided,* he is the author of *Home as Found: Authority and Genealogy in Nineteenth-Century American Literature* and has edited *American Realism: New Essays.*

Bibliography

Adams, Richard P. *Faulkner: Myth and Motion*. Princeton: Princeton University Press, 1968.

Anderson, Charles. "Faulkner's Moral Center." *Études anglaises* 7, no. 1 (January 1954): 48–58.

Aswell, Duncan. "The Recollection and the Blood: Jason's Role in *The Sound and the Fury*." *Mississippi Quarterly* 21, no. 3 (Summer 1968): 211–18.

Backman, Melvin. *Faulkner, The Major Years: A Critical Study*. Bloomington: Indiana University Press, 1966.

Bassett, John E., ed. *William Faulkner: The Critical Heritage*. London: Routledge and Kegan Paul, 1975.

———. "Family Conflict in *The Sound and the Fury*." *Studies in American Fiction* 9, no. 1 (Spring 1981): 1–20.

Baum, Catherine B. " 'The Beautiful One': Caddy Compson as Heroine of *The Sound and the Fury*." *Modern Fiction Studies* 13, no. 1 (Spring 1967): 33–44.

Bleikasten, André, ed. *William Faulkner's* The Sound and the Fury: *A Critical Casebook*. New York: Garland, 1982.

———. *The Most Splendid Failure: Faulkner's* The Sound and the Fury. Bloomington: Indiana University Press, 1976.

Bloom, Harold, ed. *Modern Critical Views: William Faulkner*. New York: Chelsea House, 1986.

Bowling, Lawrence. "Faulkner: Technique in *The Sound and the Fury*." *Kenyon Review* 10, no. 4 (Autumn 1948): 555–66.

———. "Faulkner and the Theme of Innocence." *Kenyon Review* 20, no. 3 (Summer 1958) 466–87.

Brodhead, Richard H., ed. *Faulkner: New Perspectives*. Englewood Cliffs, N.J.: Prentice-Hall, 1983.

Brooks, Cleanth. *William Faulkner: First Encounters*. New Haven: Yale University Press, 1983.

———. *William Faulkner: Toward Yoknapatawpha and Beyond*. New Haven: Yale University Press, 1973.

———. *William Faulkner: The Yoknapatawpha Country*. New Haven: Yale University Press, 1963.

———. "Primitivism in *The Sound and the Fury*." *English Institute Essays, 1952*,

151

edited by Alan S. Downer, 5–28. New York: Columbia University Press, 1954.

Brown, May Cameron. "The Language of Chaos: Quentin Compson in *The Sound and the Fury*." *American Literature* 51, no. 4 (January 1980): 544–53.

Brylowski, Walter. *Faulkner's Olympian Laugh: Myth in the Novels*. Detroit: Wayne State University Press, 1968.

Cecil, L. Moffitt. "A Rhetoric for Benjy." *Southern Literary Journal* 3, no. 1 (Fall 1970): 32–46.

Chakovsky, Sergei. "Word and Idea in *The Sound and the Fury*." In *New Directions in Faulkner Studies: Faulkner and Yoknapatawpha, 1983*, edited by Doreen Fowler and Ann J. Abadie, 283–301. Jackson: University Press of Mississippi, 1984.

Coindreau, Maurice Edgar. *The Time of William Faulkner: A French View of Modern American Fiction*, Edited and chiefly translated by George McMillan Reeves. Columbia: University of South Carolina Press, 1971.

Collins, Carvel. "The Interior Monologues of *The Sound and the Fury*." *English Institute Essays, 1952*, edited by Alan S. Downer, 29–56. New York: Columbia University Press, 1954.

Conder, John J. *Naturalism in American Fiction: The Classic Phase*. Lexington: University Press of Kentucky, 1984.

Cowan, Michael H., ed. *Twentieth-Century Interpretations of* The Sound and the Fury. Englewood Cliffs, N.J.: Prentice-Hall, 1968.

Cowley, Malcolm. "Dilsey and the Compsons." *University of Mississippi Studies in English* 14 (1974): 79–97.

Dauner, Louise. "Quentin and the Walking Shadow: The Dilemma of Nature and Culture." *Arizona Quarterly* 21, no. 2 (Summer 1965): 159–71.

Davis, Boyd. "Caddy Compson's Eden." *Mississippi Quarterly* 30, no. 3 (Summer 1977): 381–94.

Edel, Leon. "How to Read *The Sound and the Fury*." In *Varieties of Literary Experience*, edited by Stanley Burnshaw, 241–57. New York: New York University Press, 1962.

Edmonds, Irene C. "Faulkner and the Black Shadow." In *Southern Renascence: The Literature of the Modern South*, edited by Louis D. Rubin and R. D. Jacobs, 192–206. Baltimore: Johns Hopkins University Press, 1953.

Foster, Ruel E. "Social Order and Disorder in Faulkner's Fiction." *Approach* 55 (Spring 1965): 20–28.

Geffen, Arthur. "Profane Time, Sacred Time, and Confederate Time in *The Sound and the Fury*." *Studies in American Fiction* 2, no. 2 (Autumn 1974): 175–97.

Greer, Dorothy D. "Dilsey and Lucas: Faulkner's Use of the Negro as a Gauge of Moral Character." *The Emporia State Research Studies* 11, no. 1 (September 1962): 43–61.

Gresset, Michel. "Psychological Aspects of Evil in *The Sound and the Fury*." *Mississippi Quarterly* 19, no. 3 (Summer 1966): 143–53.

Hagopian, John V. "Nihilism in Faulkner's *The Sound and the Fury*." *Modern Fiction Studies* 13, no. 1 (Spring 1967): 45–56.

Hoffman, Frederick J., and Olga W. Vickery, eds. *William Faulkner: Two Decades of Criticism*. East Lansing: Michigan State College Press, 1951.

Hoffman, Frederick J., and Olga W. Vickery, eds. *William Faulkner: Three Decades of Criticism*. East Lansing: Michigan State University Press, 1960.

Howe, Irving. *William Faulkner: A Critical Study.* 3rd ed. New York: Random House, 1975.

Hunt, John W. *William Faulkner: Art in Theological Tension.* Syracuse: Syracuse University Press, 1964.

Irwin, John T. *Doubling and Incest/Repetition and Revenge: A Speculative Reading of Faulkner.* Baltimore: Johns Hopkins University Press, 1975.

Iser, Wolfgang. *The Implied Reader: Patterns of Communication from Bunyan to Beckett.* Baltimore: The Johns Hopkins University Press, 1974.

Izsak, Emily K. "The Manuscript of *The Sound and the Fury:* The Revisions in the First Section." *Studies in Bibliography* 20 (1967): 189–202.

Jehlen, Myra. *Class and Character in Faulkner's South.* New York: Columbia University Press, 1981.

Jenkins, Lee. *Faulkner and Black-White Relations: A Psychoanalytic Approach.* New York: Columbia University Press, 1981.

Kaluza, Irena. *The Functioning of Sentence Structure in the Stream-of-Consciousness Technique of William Faulkner's* The Sound and the Fury: *A Study in Linquistic Stylistics.* Krakow: Nakladem Uniwersytetu Jagiellonskiego, 1967.

Kenner, Hugh. *A Homemade World: The American Modernist Writers.* New York: Knopf, 1975.

King, Richard H. *A Southern Renaissance: The Cultural Awakening of the American South, 1930–1955.* New York: Oxford University Press, 1980.

Kinney, Arthur F. *Faulkner's Narrative Poetics: Style as Vision.* Amherst: University of Massachusetts Press, 1978.

———, ed. *Critical Essays on William Faulkner: The Compson Family.* Boston: G. K. Hall, 1982.

Kreiswirth, Martin. "Learning as He Wrote: Re-Used Materials in *The Sound and the Fury.*" *Mississippi Quarterly* 34, no. 3 (Summer 1981): 281–98.

Longley, John L., Jr. " 'Who Never Had a Sister': A Reading of *The Sound and the Fury.*" *Mosaic* 7, no. 1 (Fall 1973): 35–53.

Lowrey, Perrin. "Concepts of Time in *The Sound and the Fury.*" *English Institute Essays, 1952,* edited by Alan S. Downer, 57–82. New York: Columbia University Press, 1954.

Mellard, James M. "*The Sound and the Fury:* Quentin Compson and Faulkner's 'Tragedy of Passion'." *Studies in the Novel* 2, no. 1 (Spring 1970): 61–75.

———. "Faulkner's *Commedia:* Synecdoche and Anagogic Symbolism in *The Sound and the Fury.*" *Journal of English and German Philology* 83, no. 4 (October 1984): 534–46.

Meriwether, James B., ed. *The Merrill Studies in* The Sound and the Fury. Columbus, Ohio: Charles E. Merrill, 1970.

Messedi, Douglas. "The Problem of Time in *The Sound and the Fury:* A Critical Reassessment and Reinterpretation." *Southern Literary Journal* 6, no. 2 (Spring 1974): 19–41.

Millgate, Jane. "Quentin Compson as Poor Player: Verbal and Social Clichés in *The Sound and the Fury.*" *Revue des lanques vivantes* 34, no. 1 (1968): 40–49.

Millgate, Michael. *The Achievement of William Faulkner.* Lincoln: University of Nebraska Press, 1966.

Minter, David. "Faulkner, Childhood, and the Making of *The Sound and the Fury.*" *American Literature* 51, no. 3 (November 1979): 376–93.

Moore, Andy J. "Luster's Ordered Role in *The Sound and the Fury.*" In *American Bypaths: Essays in Honor of E. Hudson Long,* edited by Robert G. Collmer and Jack W. Herring, 167–86. Waco, Tex.: Baylor University Press, 1980.

O'Donnell, George Marion. "Faulkner's Mythology." *Kenyon Review,* 1 (1939). Reprinted in Robert Penn Warren, ed. *Faulkner: A Collection of Critical Essays.* Englewood Cliffs, N.J.: Prentice-Hall, 1966: 23–33.

Peavy, Charles D. "Faulkner's Use of Folklore in *The Sound and the Fury.*" *Journal of American Folklore* 79, no. 313 (July–September 1966): 437–47.

Pikoulis, John. *The Art of William Faulkner.* London: Macmillian, 1982.

Polk, Noel. *An Editorial Handbook for William Faulkner's* The Sound and the Fury. New York: Garland, 1985.

Powell, Sumner C. "William Faulkner Celebrates Easter, 1928." *Perspective* 2, no. 4 (Summer 1949): 195–218.

Putzel, Max. *Genius of Place: William Faulkner's Triumphant Beginnings.* Baton Rouge: Louisiana State University Press, 1985.

Reed, Joseph W., Jr. *Faulkner's Narrative.* New Haven: Yale University Press, 1973.

Rosenberg, Bruce A. "The Oral Quality of Rev. Shegog's Sermon in William Faulkner's *The Sound and the Fury.*" *Literatur in Wissenschaft und Unterricht* 2, no. 2 (1969): 73–88.

Ross, Stephen M. "The 'Loud World' of Quentin Compson." *Studies in the Novel* 7, no. 2 (Summer 1975): 245–57.

Slabey, Robert M. "The 'Romanticism' of *The Sound and the Fury.*" *Mississippi Quarterly* 16, no. 3 (Summer 1963): 146–59.

Slater, Judith. "Quentin's Tunnel Vision: Modes of Perception and Their Stylistic Realization in *The Sound and the Fury.*" *Literature and Psychology* 27, no. 1 (1977): 4–15.

Slatoff, Walter J. "*The Sound and the Fury.*" In *Quest for Failure: A Study of William Faulkner,* 149–58. Ithaca: Cornell University Press, 1960.

Snead, James A. *Figures of Division: Faulkner's Major Novels.* New York: Methuen, 1986.

Spilka, Mark. "Quentin Compson's Universal Grief." *Contemporary Literature* 11, no. 4 (Autumn 1970): 451–69.

Steward, George R., and Joseph M. Backus. " 'Each in Its Ordered Place': Structure and Narrative in 'Benjy's Section' of *The Sound and the Fury.*" *American Literature* 29, no. 4 (January 1958): 440–56.

Swiggart, Peter. "Moral and Temporal Order in *The Sound and the Fury.*" *Sewanee Review* 61, no. 2 (Spring 1953): 221–37.

Thompson, Lawrance. "Mirror Analogues in *The Sound and the Fury.*" *English Institute Essays, 1952,* edited by Alan S. Downer, 83–106. New York: Columbia University Press, 1954.

Traschen, Isodore. "The Tragic Form of *The Sound and the Fury.*" *Southern Review* 12, no. 4 (October 1976): 798–813.

Vickery, Olga. *The Novels of William Faulkner: A Critical Interpretation,* rev. ed. Baton Rouge: Louisiana State University Press, 1964.

Waggoner, Hyatt H. "William Faulkner's Passion Week of the Heart." In *The Tragic Vision and the Christian Faith,* edited by Nathan A. Scott, Jr., 306–23. New York: Association Press, 1957.

——. *William Faulkner: From Jefferson to the World*. Lexington: University of Kentucky Press, 1959.

Wagner, Linda W. "Language and Act: Caddy Compson." *Southern Literary Journal* 14 (1982): 49–61.

——. "Jason Compson: The Demands of Honor." *Sewanee Review* 79, no. 4 (Autumn 1971): 554–75.

Wall, Carey. "*The Sound and the Fury:* The Emotional Center." *Midwest Quarterly* 11, no. 4 (Summer 1970): 371–87.

Warren, Robert Penn, ed. *Faulkner: A Collection of Critical Essays*. Englewood Cliffs, N.J.: Prentice-Hall, 1966.

Weber, Robert Wilhelm. *Die Aussage der Form. Zur Textur und Struktur des Bewusstseinsromans. Darquestellt an W. Faulkners* The Sound and the Fury. Heidelberg: C. Winter, 1969.

Wilder, Amos N. *Theology and Modern Literature*. Cambridge: Harvard University Press, 1958.

Wittenberg, Judith Bryant. *Faulkner: The Transfiguration of Biography*. Lincoln and London: University of Nebraska Press, 1979.

Acknowledgments

"Doubling and Incest/Repetition and Revenge" by John T. Irwin from *Doubling and Incest/Repetition and Revenge* by John T. Irwin, © 1975 by The Johns Hopkins University Press, Baltimore/London. Reprinted by permission of The Johns Hopkins University Press.

"*The Sound and the Fury* and the Dislocation of Form" (originally entitled "*The Sound and the Fury*") by Donald M. Kartiganer from *The Fragile Thread* by Donald M. Kartiganer, © 1979 by the University of Massachusetts Press, Amherst, Mass. Reprinted by permission.

"*The Sound and the Fury:* The Search for a Narrative Method" (originally entitled "The Search for a Narrative Method") by Gary Lee Stonum from *Faulkner's Career: An Internal Literary History* by Gary Lee Stonum, © 1979 by Cornell University. Reprinted by permission of the publisher, Cornell University Press.

"*The Sound and the Fury:* A Logic of Tragedy" by Warwick Wadlington from *American Literature* 53, no. 3 (November 1981), © 1981 by Duke University Press. Reprinted by permission of the publisher, Duke University Press.

" 'Jim Crow' and *The Sound and the Fury*" (originally entitled "*The Sound and the Fury*") by Thadious M. Davis from *Faulkner's "Negro": Art and the Southern Context* by Thadious M. Davis, © 1983 by Louisiana State University Press. Reprinted by permission of Louisiana State University Press.

"The Discovery of Loss in *The Sound and the Fury*" by John T. Matthews from *The Play of Faulkner's Language* by John T. Matthews, © 1982 by Cornell University Press. Reprinted by permission of the publisher, Cornell University Press.

"Precarious Coherence: Objects through Time" by Gail L. Mortimer from *Faulkner's Rhetoric of Loss: A Study in Perception and Meaning* by Gail L. Mortimer, © 1983 by the University of Texas Press. Reprinted by permission of University of Texas Press.

"The Myth of *The Sound and the Fury*" by Eric J. Sundquist from *Faulkner: The House Divided* by Eric J. Sundquist, © 1983 by The Johns Hopkins University Press, Baltimore/London. Reprinted by permission of The Johns Hopkins University Press.

Index